The Saint
of
Beersheba

SUNY Series in Israeli Studies
Russell Stone, Editor

AND

SUNY Series in Anthropology and Judaic Studies
Walter P. Zenner, Editor

The Saint
of
Beersheba

by

Alex Weingrod

State University of New York Press

Photography by Daniel Weingrod

Published by

State University of New York Press, Albany

© 1990   State University of New York

For information, address State University of New York
Press, State University Plaza, Albany, N.Y., 12246

Library of Congress Cataloging-in-Publication Data

Weingrod, Alex
     The Saint of Beersheba/by Alex Weingrod; photography by Daniel
Weingrod.
        p.   cm. — (SUNY series in Israeli studies) (SUNY series in
anthropology and Judaic studies)
     Bibliography: p.
     Includes index.
     ISBN 0-7914-0138-3. — ISBN 0-7914-0139-1 (pbk.)
     1. Jewish pilgrims and pilgrimages — Israel — Beersheba. 2. Chouri,
Chayim, d. 1957. 3. Jewish saints — Africa, North — Biography.
4. Jewish saints — Israel — Beersheba — Biography. 5. Beersheba
(Israel) — Religious life and customs.   I. Title.   II. Series.
III. Series: SUNY series in anthropology and Judaic studies.
BM392.B42W45   1990
306'.6 — dc19   89-4047
                                                                                          CIP

10 9 8 7 6 5 4 3 2 1

Contents

INTRODUCTION   vii

Chapter 1. *Zaddik*   1
Chapter 2. Text   23
Chapter 3. Performance   47
Chapter 4. Process   69
Chapter 5. Comparison   93

NOTES   113
REFERENCES   117
FIGURES   123
INDEX   145

Introduction

This book is about a new Jewish *zaddik*, or "saint," and the pilgrimage to his grave. How a new saint and holy shrine have recently been created makes a fascinating tale, and along the way this process also illuminates some major features of present-day Israeli society and culture. What sparked the research, and how it subsequently unfolded, is a story in itself.

My interest in the saint of Beersheba began during a conversation with Issachar Ben-Ami, the Israeli folklorist who has done major documentary work on Jewish pilgrimages in Morocco and Israel. During the discussion he described a new *hillula*, or "memorial celebration," taking place at the grave of Rabbi Chayim Chouri in the Beersheba cemetery. Ben-Ami suggested that I attend the pilgrimage. I went to the cemetery and took part in this extraordinary gathering. I was engrossed (seized might be a better word) by the sheer power of what occurred there, and each year I have returned to participate in the festivities.

Throughout these years—I first attended the *hillula* in 1978—I have been trying to unravel the meanings of this complex event. Together with my students at the Ben Gurion University of the Negev I observed the pilgrimage and interviewed many of those taking part in it. There are a growing number of additional Israeli sacred shrines and pilgrimages, and I attended many of these as well. These observations and interviews were then discussed and analyzed in a series of university seminars. Members of the Chouri family took an active interest in my research; Yosef Chouri spoke to the seminar, and during the yearly celebration, he and other members of the family were always patient and cooperative.

Daniel Weingrod, then teaching photography at the Bezalel Art Academy in Jerusalem, also attended the pilgrimage and took photographs throughout the day. His photography captures the spirit of the *hillula*: joy, prayer, mystic belief, diversity, and spontaneity. Together with the written text the photographs document and interpret the varied dimensions of this exceptional celebration.

I would like to thank Yosef Chouri and members of the Chouri family for their generous guidance and advice. Some of the ideas developed in this book were first presented to seminars and other forums in departments of anthropology at a number of universities: the Ben Gurion University of the Negev, Bar Ilan University, the State University of New York at Stony Brook, Brandeis University, the Institute of Social Anthropology at Oxford University, the Cambridge University Social Anthropology Society, the Free University of Amsterdam, Digby Stuart College, and at an SSRC-sponsored conference hosted by the Institute of Advanced Studies at Princeton University. I am indebted to colleagues and friends at each of these meetings who listened patiently to my tales of this exuberant festival, and then asked probing questions. Early in the research Miri Wisnitzer brought to my attention a long list of relevant Hebrew texts and commentaries. At different times a number of colleagues were kind enough to read draft versions of this book: Henry Abromovitz, Yoram Bilu, Virginia Dominguez, Dale Eickelman, Don Handelman, Samuel Heilman, Simon Lichman, James Piscatori, the late Victor Turner, Lawrence Rosen, and Melford Spiro. I thank each of them for their many helpful suggestions. Funds from the Wenner-Gren Foundation for Anthropological Research helped to conclude the study.

Most of this manuscript was completed while I was on leave at Oxford University during the spring of 1986. I wish to thank the president and fellows of Wolfson College and Dr. David Patterson, president of the Oxford Postgraduate Centre for Hebrew Studies, for their friendship and cordiality, and also for providing so congenial an environment. Finally, my thanks to Judith Friedgut who typed the final draft of the book, and to Rosalie M. Robertson, my patient editor at SUNY Press, for her good advice and assistance.

1 Zaddik

Each year, during the spring season, large crowds gather to take part in the pilgrimage to the grave of a new Jewish saint, or *zaddik*, Rabbi Chayim Chouri. The pilgrimage itself takes place in the municipal cemetery of the city of Beersheba, located in Israel's southern Negev region. People come from all over Israel: they arrive by bus, taxi, or private car; some even come part of the way on foot, walking the last mile or two from the outskirts of the city. When they arrive they join the hundreds, and later thousands, who are packed around the rabbi's tomb. This is, to say the least, an extraordinary event.

There are a great many ancient "holy places" in the Holy Land – to cite just a few, the graves of the biblical Patriarchs in Hebron, the tomb of Rabbi Shimon bar Yochai near Safed, and, for that matter, the Western Wall, Church of the Holy Sepulcher, and Dome of the Rock in Jerusalem. Each of these (and there are a great many others) is a legendary, fabled site, richly hallowed in myth and spiritual tradition. What makes this particular grave in the Beersheba cemetery so interesting is that it is a *new* holy place. Rabbi Chouri, who had been a leading rabbi among the Jewish communities of southern Tunisia, emigrated to Israel in 1955; two years later he died and was buried in the Beersheba cemetery. Since then his tomb has become a shrine and the focus of a yearly pilgrimage. During the day thousands of persons crowd around the rabbi's grave, and the cemetery is transformed by their presence and becomes the site (to use Victor Turner's term) of a "multivocal event" that reverberates and has meanings on a series of different levels. In short, this pilgrimage is the kind of marvelously complex social event that attracts attention and invites explanation and interpretation.

To be more specific, the activities that make up this now yearly celebration pose a series of both historical and anthropological questions. The list of queries is lengthy, and they become increasingly more

1

complicated. Who was Rabbi Chouri, and what was the process by which he became a *zaddik*? Who takes part in this pilgrimage, and why do they come? What is meant by such terms as *saint* and *pilgrimage* in Jewish religious tradition, as well as for those who take part in the celebration? Why are certain distinctive cultural features expressed in the great performance that unfolds during the day, and what meaning does this event have in the lives of those who flock to the cemetery?

Some of these questions are comparatively simple to answer, while others are much more difficult. Most of this book is devoted to formulating answers to these and a number of other related topics. Broadly speaking, these are the themes pursued throughout this study — tracing the process by which a new saint and shrine literally have been created, and then conceptualizing and interpreting this set of events within the social, cultural, and political contexts of contemporary Israeli society.

This first chapter sets the stage. It combines threads that are, at once, biographical, historical, and cultural. Rabbi Chouri is the central figure, and he is presented in the background of his time and place.

II

Chayim Chouri was born in Jerba, an island off the coast of Tunisia, in 1885. For many centuries Jerba was a home for both Muslim Berbers and Jews. The Jewish legends trace their Jerban lineage back to the fifth-century B.C.E., before the destruction of the Temple in Jerusalem; their own "marvelous synagogue," the Ghriba, is said to have been built from Temple stones and a door transported from Jerusalem by refugees who had reached the island and founded a holy community there. This myth is important, for it suggests the character of Jewish life on the island. Particularly during the eighteenth and nineteenth centuries Jerba was famed as the "Jerusalem of Africa," and within its synagogues rabbis and scholars were trained who served the Jewish communities throughout North Africa. Chayim Chouri was born into this sacred ambience, and his life was deeply shaped by his Jerban upbringing.

What was life in Jerba like at the turn of the twentieth century? Fortunately, Udovitch and Valensi's fine ethnographic study, *The Last Arab Jews*, provides a poetic glimpse of the "inner life" of the Jews who lived there. During the first half of the twentieth century the Jewish population ranged from between 3000 and 4000 persons; most concentrated within the larger of the two Jewish villages, Hara Kabira, while the smaller Jewish settlement, Dighet or Hara Sghira, reputedly included within it the descendents of *Kohanim*, or "priests." Occupationally, many Jerban Jews were concentrated in the wool trade as dyers and merchants, others were craftsmen and peddlers, and still others worked as artisans in precious metals. Living in their own nearby villages, the Jerban Berbers were primarily agriculturalists and herders, and members of both groups met in the local periodic markets where goods and services were exchanged. However, what distinguished this small Jewish community was not its skilled artisanry or overland trading networks, but rather, its exceptional concentration upon religious life and learning: there were eleven synagogues in Hara Kabira, five in Hara Sghira, and together they formed the center of Jerban Jewry's "theocratic republic." Deshen, who has written extensively on the Jews of Jerba and southern Tunisia, makes the point that "there was hardly any male social activity completely beyond the context of the synagogues and traditional learning" (1982, 126), and Udovitch and Valensi draw the conclusion that a "penchant to magnify the slightest aspects of religious life" was a "distinctive feature of Jerban Judaism" (1984, 13). Jewish life in Jerba, in short, was governed by orthodoxy and tightly orchestrated by daily, monthly, and yearly religious rituals.

As one would expect, learning and a learned elite guided everyday life.

> Intimate knowledge of the Law and rigorous execution of its prescriptions seem to be the main preoccupation of these communities, and orthodoxy their dominant characteristic. . . . What endowed the two communities with their vitality is not the strength of political institutions or of official administrative organs, but rather the participation of each individual in the life of the community, and the respect and reaffirmation of each individual for its collective norms. For this purpose, public opinion confers higher authority on a single rabbi and confides in him the responsibility for interpreting the law, for arbitrating conflicts, and for serving as a general guide to the community in matters both sacred and profane. (1984, 40-41)

This concentration upon learning was all-encompassing. "Participation in the study of Talmud during the evenings was popular, on the sabbath the sages gave public sermons of various kinds and levels, and also small groups met together to study" (Deshen 1982, 126). Most striking in this regard was the emphasis given to publishing original sacred books and learned journals; Udovitch and Valensi conclude that during the past 100 years "the Jewish community of this island has produced close to five hundred published books. . . . In addition to books, for two decades, beginning in the mid-thirties, there were between three and five monthly journals published and written in Jerba" (1984, 84). Men who were artisans and merchants, as well as rabbis who were legal specialists and scholars, wrote and published these complex expositions on problems of talmudic interpretation. Printing of sacred books flourished in Jerba not so much because of the presence of Hebrew printing presses, but rather the reverse was true: presses were imported in order to publish the stream of sacred commentaries produced by members of this tiny community. This was, without doubt, the refinement of an exceptional cultural specialization.

With these features in mind we can now return to our central figure. Late in his life, when he was already in Beersheba, Rabbi Chouri wrote a brief autobiography. Although a great deal is left out, the document describes the main events of his life. His parents made their home in Hara Sghira, the smaller of the two Jerban Jewish villages. Chayim's father was born there, while his mother came from the mainland town of Gabes. He was born late in their lives, the first son following four daughters. The birth of a male child had been keenly awaited; in fact, the failure to produce a male offspring had almost led to the divorce of the future rabbi's parents. Chayim's "miraculous birth," following his mother's plaintive prayers for a son, was consequently an especially joyous and blessed event. As a youngster he was spoiled and admired by his older sisters; in the memoir he recalls that at mealtime he was served rice, while his sisters were content with the watery soup that the rice had been cooked in (Matzliach and Chadad, n. d., 15).

Like all of the Jewish males in Hara Sghira, Chouri began his religious studies at an early age. This was a period of particular cultural flowering; one of his contemporaries, Rabbi Moshe Khalfon Hacohen, would soon begin his massive work of legal codification, and the Jerban synagogues and yeshivoth ("religious academies") were intense centers of scholarly work (Udovitch and Valensi 1984). The young Chayim showed special promise—he came under the personal guidance of Rabbi David Hacohen, a leading local scholar, and he was also a favorite of the then head of the religious court, Rabbi Zaken Moshe

Mazuz. He received his *smichah*, or "ordination as a rabbi," at the age of eighteen, and continued his studies for another two years. "I was then asked to teach students in Gabes," he writes cryptically in his memoir. For the next fifty or so years Rabbi Chouri divided his time between Jerba and Gabes.

Chouri's rabbinic career developed rapidly. He remained only briefly in Gabes — he missed his home and the intensity of the Jerban seminaries — and shortly thereafter he returned to Hara Sghira. His special talents were gaining wider recognition. Gifted with a sonorous voice, he was well-known as a *chazan*, or "cantor," and his dramatic Sabbath sermons and homilies drew crowds of women as well as men ("women crowded into the women's loft of the synagogue to hear him"). Moreover, his reputation as a talmudic sage and teacher also brought him a growing number of students. While still a young man, he was appointed to the three-member religious court in Hara Sghira; this was certainly a mark of high esteem from his rabbinic peers. Then, in the mid-1920s, the position of chief rabbi of Gabes became vacant and was offered to him. He was reluctant to again leave his beloved Jerba, but following prolonged negotiations ("I will only teach twenty-five students, in one class, and in a new building") he finally accepted the post.

Ninety miles from Jerba, and with its population of approximately 3000 Jews, Gabes was the largest Jewish community in southern Tunisia. The chief rabbi also served the many small communities of Jews sprinkled across the south Tunisian countryside. As Chacham Bashi, or chief rabbi, Chouri was responsible for overseeing all of the local communal institutions, as well as representing the Jewish community before the secular state authorities. For nearly three decades he was actively engaged in the daily life of Jews throughout this region. He appears to have been an energetic executive and initiator of projects; he organized and supported numerous charitable institutions both in Gabes and Jerba, arranged for the building of a special inn for Jewish travelers, and was especially active in printing and distributing a lengthy list of religious books written by himself and his Jerban colleagues. ("In all of Tunisia no one could match him in his ability to print, bind, and finally sell religious books.") Apart from these projects, Rabbi Chouri was also involved in a wide range of other activities. He continued to teach advanced classes of students in Gabes, and his Sabbath and Holy Day sermons, often delivered in Jerba as well as in Gabes, always drew large crowds. He took a special interest in those who had fallen upon hard times and was known for his ability to develop close ties with persons from all walks of life. The rabbi's spiritual powers were famous; an old photograph shows him seated on the ground, his right hand placed upon the brow of a supplicant who had come to him for his blessing. Above all, he was a popular figure. "It was enough to write the words 'the rabbi is here' on the synagogue entrance, and all would come to welcome him."

Gabes and southern Tunisia seemed to be an insular area, remote from turbulence and social upheavals. Still, the long period of French colonial rule brought changes even to rural zones such as these. For example, with improving health care and economic conditions the Jewish communities grew in size, and the entrance of secular French culture also challenged the entrenched religious orthodoxy. Moreover, a series of more momentous changes soon began to unfold. During the Second World War German divisions moved into Tunisia, and for a brief period of time (November 1942 until May 1943) the Germans and the Vichy French ruled Tunisia. This was a difficult, frightening period for the Jews. Both in Tunis, the capital and largest population center, and in other cities throughout the country, Jews were harassed and often attacked by the German occupiers. Hundreds of Jews were brought to so-called labor camps where they were forced to work for the occupiers; many others were rounded up, registered, and required to wear a yellow Star of David, money was exorted from them, and Jewish communal buildings were frequently vandalized (Abitbol 1982). German military detachments also reached Gabes, and as head of the Jewish community, Rabbi Chouri was responsible for negotiating with them. His diplomatic skills were often tested by the German threats; they demanded corvées of forced labor, ransom in gold or precious jewels, as well as lodging and food. Rabbi Chouri was successful in these difficult encounters — although there were repeated threats and demands, in Gabes and in the nearby towns the Jews were not preyed upon by the German occupiers.

For the Jews of Tunisia the most significant changes began to take place following the establishment of Israel in 1948. Even earlier, already in the early 1920s, a Tunisian Zionist movement had been formed, and in the decades that followed a small number of Tunisian Jews had made their way to Palestine. The enthusiasm for immigration grew as the news of Israel's creation spread throughout the Jewish communities; in addition, the clashes that then broke out between Muslims and Jews in Tunisia also led many to decide to leave for the Jewish state. The city of Tunis became the main center of immigration activities; the Jewish Agency, who organized the immigration, had its offices there, and the immigrants were registered and sent out from the capital city. Many of the Jews of Gabes and Jerba joined in this immigration movement—sooner or later practically everyone was caught up in the fever to leave. Indeed, by the mid-1960s nearly all of the Jews of southern Tunisia had left the country. True to their ancient traditions, the Jews of Jerba were among the last to leave. Udovitch and Valensi titled their study of Jerban Jewry *The Last Arab Jews*, but even there, in what had for centuries been the "Jerusalem of Africa," the Jewish community dwindled to several hundred families.

Rabbi Chouri took an active part in the immigration movement. He had long been identified as a Zionist; in fact, in his youth he had been a member of a Zionist group in Jerba. However, as chief rabbi of Gabes he felt obliged to remain in the town as long as other Jews were still there. At the same time, he encouraged members of his own family to leave for Israel. Beginning in 1948, his four sons emigrated, and later his wife and daughters joined them. Rabbi Chouri remained in Gabes until 1955. By that time most of the Jews had emigrated from Tunisia, and he, too, decided to leave and join his family. He was driven by car from Gabes to Tunis, where he boarded a plane and flew first to Rome and from there, finally, to Tel Aviv. His family and close friends met him at the airport: photos show him descending from the plane followed by bemused Israeli officials who seem to be taken aback by the enthusiastic crowd that had gathered to greet "their rabbi."

Rabbi Chouri's wife and most of the children had in the meantime settled in Beersheba. For a short time following his arrival he stayed with his eldest son, himself a rabbi and teacher, in Bnai Brak, a small orthodox religious town close to Tel Aviv. Soon thereafter he joined his family in Beersheba; they lived together in a modest home on the edge of this bustling new town, and he spent his time in quiet study, prayer, and visits with friends. As previously in Gabes, his home in Israel became something of a center for the local Tunisian community. Two years after his arrival in Israel, on May 28, 1957, he fell ill and died. Rabbi Chouri was seventy-two-years-old at the time of his death.

These are, in broad outline form, the main contours of Rabbi Chouri's life. They delineate a person of considerable learning, energetic leadership, and great personal warmth. His activities as chief rabbi of Gabes, plus his continuous contacts with the small rural Jewish villages as well as the Jerban communities, made him a well-known, widely-respected person. He had performed marriages, delivered sermons, eulogized the dead, welcomed visitors, and delivered legal judgments continuously over a period of nearly five decades. Certainly he was a popular figure — he was simply "haRav," "the rabbi," for the 8000 or 9000 Jews who had lived in the towns and villages of southern Tunisia.

It is also important to add several personal notes. Rabbi Chouri was married twice. His first wife died, leaving him with two daughters. He later remarried and had eleven children with his second wife, but only six of them — four sons and two daughters — survived to become adults. Finally a word regarding his physical appearance. Photographs show him to be a broad, imposing figure, full bearded and possessed of deep-set eyes and a broad nose. Dressed in a sash, and with a turban on his head, his regal gaze set him off from others. As he aged, his beard turned white and his face became wider and softer. The total effect was, indeed, that of a *zaddik*, or "saintly person."

Rabbi Chouri's death was briefly reported in the Israeli press, and his funeral was attended by a small group that included family members and Tunisian Jews who came from all parts of Israel. He was buried in the Beersheba municipal cemetery, in a grave-plot set along the western edge of the large field that had been turned into the city's cemetery. It was at first a plain burial site, although later, as we shall see, it was considerably enlarged and adorned.

In Jewish tradition it is customary for family members and friends to gather at the grave on the anniversary of the deceased's death. The following year members of the Chouri family and a small handful of friends again gathered at the grave site; several of his rabbinic colleagues recalled the rabbi's deeds during his life, and one of his sons then recited the *kaddish* prayer. They came again the next year and the year thereafter, each time in larger numbers. Seven years after his death, in 1964, the newspapers estimated that a crowd of 10,000 persons took part in the celebration. In this way the *hillula* of Rabbi Chayim Chouri became established and, over the years, grew enormously in size. He was on the way to becoming "the saint of Beersheba."

III

Before continuing, it is important to explain and clarify several of the terms that are being used, as well as the overall context of the event. The term *pilgrimage* has been employed when referring to the crowds of persons who journey to the rabbi's grave on the anniversary of his death. In the previous paragraph, however, a different word — *hillula* — was introduced. What do these terms mean? What is the difference between a *pilgrimage* and a *hillula*? In addition, what is meant by the term *zaddik*, translated here as "saint"? How, if at all, do saints enter into Jewish religious traditions?

The term *pilgrimage* is rendered in Hebrew as *aliya l'regel*, literally, "going up by foot." The reference is biblical and depicts the Israelites who three times each year (on the festivals of Pesach, Shevuoth, and Succoth) "went up by foot" to Jerusalem to celebrate at the Temple. The commandment clearly stated: "Three times a year shall all thy males appear before the Lord thy God in the place which he shall choose, in the feast of unleavened bread, and in the feast of weeks, and in the feast of tabernacles" (Deuteronomy 16:16). The pilgrims (in Hebrew, *oleh regel*) were mainly men, although women also took part in the festivities, and during the exuberant Second Temple Period they came not only from nearby Judea and Galilee, but also from more distant diaspora communities. For example, Philo of Alexandria writes that "countless multitudes from countless cities come to the Temple at every festival, some by land and others by sea, from east and west and north and south" (Encyclopedia of Judaica 1971, Vol. 13, 511). As described in the Bible, these celebrations were impressive and joyful, combining thousands of persons in song, dance, prayer, and animal sacrifice. In Jerusalem itself the Temple priests organized the performances and rituals. "The essence of the pilgrimage was the entry of the individual, or the group, into the Temple to worship there and the offering of the obligatory sacrifices" (Ibid., 511). These were enthusiastic, sacred moments: the great crowds and pageantry combined to produce a sense of brotherhood as well as the knowledge of having fulfilled a religious commandment.

The Roman conquest of Judea, the destruction of the Temple, and the expulsion of the Jews in the year 70 A.D. brought an end to this specific tradition of pilgrimage. In this particular form it is a practice that has never again been revived; during the period of Roman rule, as well as under later Muslim and Christian control, small bands of Jewish pilgrims continued to travel to Jerusalem on the festivals or other holidays, but with the Temple destroyed these were occasions for mourning rather than joy. The pilgrims might pray at the Temple ruins, but these were the spontaneous acts of believers rather than the organized processions of biblical days.

Nevertheless, over many centuries the journeys of Jewish pilgrims did continue, albeit in different form. During the Middle Ages, the term referred primarily to individuals and small bands of Jews who traveled to the Holy Land from diaspora Jewish communities located in the Middle East and later in Europe. Jerusalem, ever-romantic and compelling, was a primary goal for these pilgrims, but festivals and celebrations were not their main object. Some of these travelers (*masaot* in Hebrew) were lively men who sought adventure, while others were mystics inspired by the vision of directly experiencing the sacred soil of the Holy Land. Once they had arrived in Palestine they journeyed to biblical sites such as the Cave of the Patriarchs near Hebron, or to places reputed to be the graves of famed rabbis and scholars (Vilnai 1963). Indeed, a high point of their travels was the moment when they might lie directly—prostrate themselves—upon these graves and pray for Israel's redemption (*l 'hishtateyach al kivrei kdoshim*). They spent days and often nights in prayer and reflection at the grave sites. Sometimes they were alone, but on other occasions they joined small groups of local Jewish residents who regularly went out to these holy shrines. The pilgrimage, in other words, was expressed both in the journey to the Holy Land and in travels and prayer at particular holy places.

Although there are certain obvious similarities with the pilgrimage, the tradition of *hillula* is considerably different. The origins of the *hilluloth* (plural) are to be found in both the apparently ancient Middle Eastern tendency to sanctify the graves of "holy men" and also in the specifically Jewish mystic practices that were inspired by the Kabbala, that collection of mystical writings fashioned by the rabbinic *mikubalim* of Safad in the fourteenth and fifteenth centuries. In regard to the former, gatherings or pilgrimages to "holy places" are an antique tradition everywhere in the Middle East and North Africa. The *ziyara*, a pilgrimage to the grave of a *wali*, a miracle-working saint or holy man, for many centuries has been incorporated within Muslim belief and practice throughout this region of the world.

> The graves of saints are visited as sacred places for worship. . . .
> It was believed that through the pilgrimage to the grave, prayers
> said there, and votive offerings, one could obtain his intercession
> on behalf of the petitioners. . . . Thus the distressed man, the
> woman in her domestic sorrows, in illness, poverty, etc., turns to
> the grave of the saint." (Goldziher 1971, 281)

Pilgrims or those in distress might visit the shrine on any day of the
year; in addition, popular celebrations involving crowds of believers
commonly took place on the anniversay of the *wali's* birth (*mawlid*).
Ziyaras were festive occasions, combining prayers at the graveside with
feasting, informal markets, and various entertainments.

These frequent, convivial events were incorporated into the traditions of the various groups living in the region — Jews and Christians
as well as Muslims. Indeed, in not a small number of instances the
same shrine was "claimed" by both Jews and Muslims, each of whom
called it by a different name and held their festivities on different days
(Ben Ami 1984; Voinot 1949). In this sense (as well as in others) the
Jewish tradition of *hillula* both parallels and was modeled after the
Muslim *ziyara*.

Hilluloth also have their specifically Jewish origins. The word
itself is Aramaic and literally means "festivity," "celebration," and even
more specifically, a "wedding celebration." The usual translation to
English is "memorial celebration." The inspiration for the *hillula* was
drawn from the same mystic religious sources that led to the Kabbala
and the Zohar, books of Jewish mystical belief and practice. What is
involved are, again, "holy men" in "holy places." Deshen depicts the
events graphically.

> The *hillulot* originally focused upon the death of especially pious
> men, a death that was seen to be a mystical union between the
> soul of the deceased and the God-head. . . . According to the rab-
> bis, the anniversary of the death of such powerful persons pro-
> vided a unique opportunity to discover hidden sacred secrets. For
> this reason the anniversary was marked by study, introspection
> and prayer. (1977, 110)

The *hillula* might be conducted in a home or a synagogue where
the faithful gathered to study and pray. More frequently, however, the
place of gathering became the grave itself: the *hassidim*, or "followers,"
gathered at the grave of the holy man and remained there in study
and prayer throughout the day and night.

Over time this tradition developed new and quite different meanings. The element of study declined, while popular expressions of joy and pleas for intervention expanded. The grave was conceived of as belonging to the *zaddik*, a pious man or saint, and the site itself was thought to possess special powers. Indeed, the grave became a shrine, a place where mystical forces were concentrated. Some of the *hilluloth* attracted large numbers of pilgrims.

> According to popular thought the belief developed that the *zaddik* (saint) in whose memory the celebration was held would intervene with God on behalf of his followers. Accordingly, persons who suffered from physical or mental illnesses might undertake a pilgrimage to the site of the *hillula* in the hope and belief that their suffering would be lessened. (Deshen 1977, 110-111)

Food and drink also became important elements in this popular celebration; a *hillula* is marked by a "memorial feast" at which the participants drink and eat in a holiday spirit. *Hilluloth* tend to be exuberant, joyful events—"wedding celebrations"—during which a sense of exaltation and mystical union becomes pervasive.

To summarize briefly, a *hillula* is a certain kind of pilgrimage. The celebration marks the anniversary of the death of a pious man or *zaddik*, and it typically (but not always) takes place at his grave. Some of those who attend may pray or study, but many also come to the grave to ask for the *zaddik's* help or intervention. Historically, these *hilluloth* became an important feature of what can be thought of as "popular Jewish religious expression"; while the rabbinic authorities, the guardians of orthodoxy, might oppose or criticize these celebrations, they were enthusiastically accepted by a great many persons.

This brings us to a key point: the crowds that flock to the cemetery on the anniversary of the death of Rabbi Chayim Chouri are attending a *hillula*. Indeed, the placards that announce the event describe it in these terms: *Hillulat Harav* Chayim Chouri. The events of the day need to be understood within this framework of meaning and practice.

In addition, the concept of the *zaddik* needs some further explication. In previous pages the term was translated to mean a "pious man or saint." A more literal translation might be a "righteous man," or in Hebrew, *Ish zaddik*. All three of these translations are correct—a *zaddik* is a person known during his lifetime to have been pious, saintly, and righteous. A second Hebrew term is often used together with *zaddik* — the word *kadosh*, meaning a holy person, is frequently interchanged with *zaddik*. *Ha'kadosh* or *ha'zaddik*, means a holy, saintly, righteous person, almost always a male, and in most instances a rabbi or other learned person.

Like the Muslim *wali* and the North African *marabout*, the *zaddik* is not just pious and righteous, but in addition he also exercises special powers. Principal among these are the capacity to influence events; a *zaddik* possesses *baraka*, loosely translated to mean "grace," "blessing," "spiritual force," and "charisma." Bilu puts it succinctly: "The saints were charismatic rabbis, distinguished by their erudition and piety, who were believed to possess a special spiritual force" (1987, 285). It is this "special force" that permitted them to effectively pronounce blessings upon the sick or distraught, and most important, to intercede with God on behalf of those who pray to them for assistance. This capacity to intervene is surely a major defining feature: the believers appeal to the *zaddik* to use his power and influence in order to grant their requests or resolve their dilemmas. These special capacities were recognized and made legitimate in classical Jewish tradition. The Talmud decrees that "the saints are to be considered greater than the ministering angels," and again, if *zaddikim* "desired they could create a world."

Dreams and visions are important modes of discourse between the *zaddik* and those who appeal to him for help: the believers typically relate that they saw the saint in a dream, and that he instructed them regarding the actions to take so that their wishes would be realized; or how, in moments of extreme trial and danger, the saintly presence mysteriously appeared and guided them to safety (Bilu 1987, 307). While for those who gather at the shrine there is no doubt that the *zaddik*'s powers exist, there also is no clear explanation of the specific ways in which these forces are martialed and made effective. Kabbalists and others may have speculated upon these weighty matters, but they were of little concern to the believers: for them the critical matter is that the *zaddik* has, for whatever reasons and according to whatever unknown processes, powers that are miraculous. This is, in fact, the central point: as various commentators have correctly emphasized, the ability to perform miracles is the true sign of the *zaddik* (Ben Ami 1984; Bilu 1987). This capacity to influence events in wondrous ways—to heal the sick, avert danger, or protect the innocent—is what distinguished the *zaddik* from all the others. To put it differently, the graves of most righteous Jews remain simple burial places, but for those who are believed able to perform miraculous acts their graves may become powerful holy shrines.

These beliefs and practices spread widely and deeply among Jewish communities throughout the Muslim world: to cite several examples, Syrian Jews regularly conducted *hilluloth* at the graves of famed local rabbis, just as in Palestine Jews also prayed and feasted at the graves of holy sages (Zenner 1965; Vilnai 1963). However, it was among North African Jewish communities in particular that the veneration of saints had its most exuberant growth; *zaddikim* and their *hilluloth* were a major focus within North African Jewish religious traditions. This obviously is a critical point, and it needs to be spelled out in some detail.

To begin with, Islam as it evolved in the Maghreb placed special emphasis upon saints and their powers, both spiritual and temporal. Maraboutism was, as a large number of excellent studies have shown, a major motif and generating force within Moroccan Islam in particular (Eickelman 1976; Geertz 1968; Gellner 1969; Westermark 1926). The main contours of this religious power are succinctly defined in the following passage:

> The most striking feature of North African Islam is the presence of marabouts. . . . They are persons, living or dead, to whom is attributed a special relation toward God which makes them particularly well placed to serve as intermediaries with the supernatural and to communicate God's grace (*baraka*) to their clients. . . . A concrete indication of this is the proliferation of maraboutic shrines throughout the Maghreb. . . . In Morocco's rural areas, one rarely loses sight of the squat, whitewashed, and — in the case of the more popular ones — domed maraboutic shrines. In towns, more lavish shrines with green-tiled roofs are often found. (Eickelman 1976, 7)

These shrines were typically the reputed graves of deceased marabouts: they became pilgrimage points, and the more famous among them grew into pilgrimage centers, small towns where persons came throughout the year to pray at the graveside and receive the blessings of the saint's living descendents. Each of the saints had a yearly festival (*musem*) during which time the shrine would be packed with enthusiastic crowds. This fervor and belief in the saints' miraculous powers was periodically criticized by the orthodox Muslim theologians — and yet for many North Africa Muslims maraboutism was a vital center of their religious belief system.

Given this vibrant setting of symbol and action, it is hardly surprising that many of these cultural understandings and practices were also shared by the Jewish minority. There were, quite literally, hundreds of holy sites—nearly all of them the real or reputed graves of famed rabbis—where Jews went regularly to pray for the zaddik's intercession; Ben Ami, the Israeli folklorist who has done the major documentary work on zaddikim in Morocco, lists more than 600 Jewish saints and their shrines, including dozens that were claimed by both Muslims and Jews (1984). The shrines were typically located within the Jewish cemetery, although in some cases they were in a "special spot, for example, a cave" located close to the cemetery (Goldberg 1983, 65). A zaddik's grave was usually covered by a simple roof in order to "distinguish it from other graves," but these decorations were nowhere as elaborate as the tombs of famed marabouts. Practically every Jewish community, no matter how tiny or remote, had its "own zaddik," and in some places several local saints and shrines were recognized. The identity of the saints varied: some "were well-known historical figures, at times founders or descendents of veritable dynasties of tzaddikim ... while others, of unclear historical identification, seemed to be legendary figures" (Bilu 1987, 286). A number of the saints and their shrines became particularly famous; the best example is the grave of Rabbi David u-Moshe located near Agouim in the Moroccan High Atlas mountains. Thus, as Ben Ami has shown, not only were the graves of zaddikim to be found in virtually every Jewish community, there was a kind of hierarchy of saints in which some attained regional and almost national levels of fame (Ben Ami 1984).

Believers and those in dispair or urgent need often visited the zaddik's grave throughout the year. However, the yearly hillula, performed on the anniversary of the saint's death, brought together great crowds of persons.

> In the case of the more renowned saints thousands of pilgrims from various regions would flock around the tomb in a formidable spectacle during which they feasted on slaughtered cattle, drank arak (mahia), danced and chanted, prayed and lit candles. All these activities, combining marked spirituality and high ecstasy with flesh and blood concerns, in a relaxed, at times frivolous, picnic-like atmosphere, were conducted in honor of the tzaddik. (Bilu 1987, 286)

These festivities often lasted several days; camping in tents or other makeshift quarters, the pilgrims joined together in prayer, song, feasts, and dance in and around the holy shrine. These were high points of the year, occasions for entire families and communities to celebrate together.

Several additional points need to be briefly mentioned. First, although many of the saints were historical or mythical figures, the process of identifying or "creating" new *zaddikim* continued during this century; for example, Ben Ami lists a number of new saints and sites that emerged in the 1930s and 1940s (1981, 171). This is obviously important, since among other things it indicates that these traditions remained powerful in the lives of many North African Jews. Second, even though much of the documentation presented here refers to Morocco, *zaddikim* and their *hilluloth* were also prominent within Tunisian Jewish communities. To be more specific, Udovich and Valensi have described the great *hillula* that took place each year at the Ghirba synagogue in Jerba, and Jerban Jews and others also took part in the *hillula* of Sidi Youssef al-Ma'rabi at Al-Hama, near Gabes (1984, 75, 125).

Finally, a brief comparative note is in place. Belief in the wonder-working *zaddik* is not limited to the Jewish communities that developed within Islamic civilizations, but was present as well in the traditions of European Jews. Saints, and to a lesser extent, *hilluloth*, were also found among the Ashkenazic *hassidic zaddikim* who emerged in Poland and Lithuania during the eighteenth and nineteenth centuries. As Scholem has shown, within this mystic, revivalist Jewish religious movement emphasis was placed upon the personality of the *zaddik*, the saint and leader who gathered around him a following of *hassidim*, followers and enthusiasts (1954, 325-50). The *zaddik*, who achieved contact with God through mystical means, could also perform miracles; in Scholem's words, he combined "the magician's claim to work miracles with his amulet, or through other magical practices, and the mystical enthusiasm which seeks no object but God" (Ibid, 349). To be sure, *zaddikim* in Poland and Morocco were by no means identical—but they spring from some of the same sources and express certain common features.

IV

The question, of course, is how Rabbi Chouri became a *zaddik*. During his lifetime he surely had been a learned, pious, and popular leader of his people—but a *zaddik*? What was the process by which he became known as a saint, and how was his grave transformed into a shrine where large throngs celebrated his *hillula*?

The details, as far as they can be accurately reconstructed, are as follows. (Some of the facts were presented earlier, but it is important to repeat them again so that the entire process can be properly understood). Rabbi Chouri died in the late spring of 1957 at the age of seventy-two. His funeral was attended by a small crowd of family members, old friends, and fellow Tunisans. He was buried in an ordinary grave site in the Beersheba municipal cemetery. It appears that no special attention was given to selecting the site of his grave; although the rabbi's tomb is not entirely surrounded by other gravestones, it is also not separated from the rest of the graves in the cemetery. This is a significant point, as we shall shortly see.

The *hillula* then burst ahead with astonishing speed. A year after the rabbi's death a group of family members and friends gathered at his grave. One of the rabbi's sons recited the *kaddish* prayer for the dead, and brief talks were given in his memory. Then, at some time during the following year, the idea of organizing a *hillula* to honor the rabbi was first broached. This idea was discussed by the rabbi's sons and his son-in-law, as well as among members of the local Beersheba Tunisian community. The sons and son-in-law took the initiative. Three of the sons were then working in local factories or other businesses and the fourth was attached to a *yeshiva* in another town; the son-in-law was himself a rabbi who was then living in Beersheba. A close friend of the family was employed in the Beersheba municipal offices, and he was particularly enthusiastic and helpful. This tiny group, together with several other local Tunisians, began to plan the first *hillula*. A report in a local newspaper described the festival's rapid evolution.

> The year following the Rabbi's death the idea of organizing the "*hillula* of the Negev" and of making a pilgrimage to the grave on the anniversary of his death, began to take shape. The first year some tens of persons came, just a small group of his relatives and acquaintances. But then, the very next year, large crowds began to stream there. By the following year and ever since then, it has become fixed as a tradition. (*Hedi HaDarom* 1966)

Was it really all so quick and simple? Did this now-massive yearly pilgrimage with its thousands of participants begin with just a few family members and fellow enthusiasts? The answer clearly seems to be yes: the *hillula* was initiated by a mere handful of dedicated persons, and then almost immediately it "began to take shape" and become established.

The rabbi's sons and a few friends provided the impetus and the energy. The basis for their appeal to take part in a new *hillula* was clear. During his lifetime Rabbi Chouri had been widely known and revered by several generations of South Tunisians; most of them had immigrated to Israel, and by the late 1950s probably as many as 1000 Tunisian families were living in Beersheba and a number of nearby small towns and agricultural villages. Rabbi Chouri had visited these places while he was still alive, and during his brief years in Beersheba he had also taken an interest in the affairs of former Tunisians living in Israel. The plan to have a new *hillula* honoring "their rabbi" was therefore welcomed within the Tunisian community. As the second and subsequent anniversaries of his death grew closer, the Chouri family and their friends invited their fellow Tunisians to attend the observance. The message was spread by word of mouth at the local Tunisian synagogues, at festive events and in casual conversations. They also invited the leading Tunisian rabbis to take part, and let it be known that these well-known dignitaries would attend.

In addition, already at this early stage some local Moroccan Jews began to take an interest and attended the rabbi's *hillula*. In contrast with the Tunisians who are a relatively small community, Moroccan Jews are a large *edah*, or "ethnic group," both in Beersheba and in other towns and villages throughout the Negev region and all of Israel. As we have seen, the *hillula* tradition was popular and widespread in Morocco, and it took little time for these Moroccan Jews to eagerly take part in Rabbi Chouri's rapidly developing memorial celebration. Like the Tunisians, so, too, for the Moroccans the *hillula* struck responsive chords of nostalgia and mystical enthusiasm. In effect, these Moroccans were on the way to "adopting" Rabbi Chouri; it was their growing participation that over the years has transformed this small family gathering into a much more massive event.

The Tunisian sponsors were also successful in enlisting the interest and assistance of several Beersheba city officials. Through their friend in the municipality (himself a fellow Tunisian) they requested help from the city authorities in publicizing the gathering and helping to keep order during the day. At an early stage the city officials agreed to assist with the technical details of organization. The then mayor of the city, David Touvyahu, attended the celebration in the cemetery. A photo taken in 1960 shows Touvyahu standing stiffly next to the rabbi's grave, his head covered with a cloth fedora, surrounded by bearded Tunisian rabbis and a joyous congregation. Touvyahu's patronage of the *hillula* was unusual for its time. He was a member of the reigning Israeli Ashkenazi political and cultural elite, and in those days it was not fashionable (as it has since become) for national leaders to take part in Middle Eastern ethnic festivals. Beersheba was at that time already beset by ethnic political-party factionalism, and he may have seen his attendance as a way to gather support among the growing number of North African voters; or perhaps he was intrigued by this unusual event that was developing in his city. Whatever the reasons, his presence and sponsorship no doubt also contributed to the *hillula*'s success.

Looking back, it is fair to conclude that members of the Chouri family played the role of impressario and cultural entrepreneur: during the first years they busied themselves with inviting dignitaries to the celebration, organized a public committee that improved and beautified the site, saw to it that posters announcing the *hillula* were distributed throughout the region, and so forth. Several of the brothers, and in particular the youngest, Yosef, have continued to perform these duties. Several months before the *hillula* Yosef sends out notices, contacts the authorities regarding improving the fence around the grave site, and invites leading rabbis to attend the Sabbath prayers prior to the pilgrimage. Moreover, the Chouri brothers are exceptionally busy during the *hillula* itself: throughout the day they stand next to the grave and pronouce blessings, sell candles and magical string, and generally concern themselves with the smooth running of the day's events. The fact that the *hillula* has grown only increases their worries and duties.

Yet if they are "entrepreneurs," this has over the years been a part-time vocation at best. Yosef, the most active of the brothers, was for many years employed in a factory in Beersheba; his organizational activities on behalf of the *hillula* were performed after work. (More recently, since 1982, he has been working in the Beersheba *yeshiva*, or religious seminary, that bears Rabbi Chouri's name.) All of the others who have devoted themselves to the *hillula*—brothers, brother-in-law and friends—have been voluntary, part-time activists. *Devotion* accurately expresses their activities: they are all modest, direct men, and while their personal social status may have grown with the *hillula*, they have not gained tangible economic or political advantage. The entrepreneurial tasks have not, in other words, given them much in the way of clear benefit.

These remarks lead to a broader conclusion. There certainly is an organizational component to the pilgrimage, but it is modest at best. The *hillula* is not a "promotion" (to use the advertising jargon) nor does it rest upon shrewd direction. Fundamentally it is, or represents, an outpouring of genuine belief and emotion; from the outset it has been a naive, spontaneous event, generated from complicated wellsprings that include (at the least) both belief in mystic powers and a desire to publicly demonstrate identification with one's ethnic group. This is why it has attracted thousands of participants. The printed posters announcing the event are a helpful reminder, but a great many persons would come whether or not they saw the placards. In brief, the *hillula* may have been initiated by a few persons, but its wide appeal rests upon much broader social and spiritual bases.

This conclusion is strengthened by considering again the matter of the rabbi's place of burial. It will be recalled that Rabbi Chouri was buried on the edge of the cemetery next to other graves. As was emphasized previously, this site was selected without much deliberation. However, as the *hillula* grew in popularity, it became clear that the location posed a great many problems. The hundreds and later thousands of persons taking part in the pilgrimage poured over the surrounding graves; in some cases families complained that graves of dear ones buried nearby were being damaged or defaced. It proved difficult to control the crowd, even after a fence was built around the tomb. Moreover, once the grave was perceived to be a holy place the entire site seemed inappropriate: there was not enough space to expand the shrine properly and thereby make it more impressive and dignified. For this reason as well, the Chouri family wished to transfer the shrine outside of the cemetery and rebury the *zaddik* in a separate plot across the road. The family presented a written request to the Israeli rabbinic authorities that permission be granted to move the bodily remains and the grave several hundred yards westward to a new location that would be slightly higher and stand alone. The response was negative, however: the rabbinic authorities ruled that reburial was not proper since it was forbidden by biblical injunction. Moreover, they added, how would the souls of those buried close to the rabbi (and thereby benefiting from his personal power) respond if their beloved rabbi was taken away from them? This settled the issue: the shrine was not moved, although a number of additional improvements were later made to the original burial place.

The point is that neither the Chouri family nor their friends imagined that the grave would become the focus for a giant *hillula*. When the rabbi died no one thought that his grave would become a holy shrine. Had they known that Rabbi Chouri was to be a *zaddik* they would have more carefully selected the place of burial. The entire process was—to repeat the phrase once again—naive and spontaneous.

This brings us, inevitably, to the final question: why Rabbi Chouri? Why did he become a *zaddik*?

The question is difficult, and the answers are speculative. They fall into two parts. First, already during his lifetime Rabbi Chouri was famed and revered: his accomplishments as a talmudic scholar and teacher, as well as his close personal ties over many years with many persons, made him a popular as well as respected figure. His physical appearance and demeanor also expressed a saintly quality. In other words, he fit rather easily into the mold of a *zaddik*.

This is persuasive reasoning; but it is not entirely convincing. Rabbi Chouri's scholarship may have been productive, but he can scarcely be numbered among the great talmudists. The fact that he was a popular figure also does not distinguish him from several others among his Tunisian rabbinic peers. Moreover, there is little to indicate that during his lifetime he was known to possess miraculous powers: he was consulted by those who suffered from misfortune or in regard to community issues, but there is no indication that his wisdom or personality were believed to have special or supernatural qualities.

Then why did *he* become a *zaddik*? This brings us to the second part of the answer. Rabbi Chouri's fame grew after his death. This is the common pattern in the North African Jewish tradition—in most instances the *zaddik* was recognized as possessing mystical powers following his death. The tales of miraculous acts performed by him were told after his death and while his *hillula* was growing in size. The time or period was instrumental in this process. That is, Rabbi Chouri was the first of the rabbis of wide reputation to have been buried in the Beersheba cemetery. Had he not been the first (several others have since been buried there) then his *hillula* might not have developed its large following, and his fame would at best have been minor. For a variety of reasons (these are discussed in the chapters that follow) the time was propitious for new Israeli *hilluloth* to be established. Even the date was well timed — the late spring season corresponds with a wide range of festivities including Israel Independence Day and the Lag B'Omer pilgrimage to Meron — and the new Chouri *hillula* was easily included in what has become an intensive festival period. Finally, the success of his celebration was also aided by the absence or dearth of pilgrimage sites in the Beersheba region. This is a curious but highly relevant fact: whereas the north of Israel is rich in holy places, there are few such traditional shrines in the southern part of the country. The northern Israeli towns of Safad, Tiberias, and Hatzor could boast their saints and holy places (the graves of Rabbi Shimon bar Yochai, Meir Baal Haness, and Choni Hameagel respectively) but where could one turn in the south? This was also a factor in creating this new "*hillula* of the Negev."

Rabbi Chayim Chouri became a *zaddik* following his death. The tales of miracles that he performed and the special powers that he possessed have grown since his burial in the Beersheba cemetery. Who does not know how he saved the Jews of Gabes from the hated Germans by performing wonderful miracles or how he appears in dreams and gently explains to believers how they can rid themselves of some ailment or affliction? Such tales (and many others) are now collected in books and repeated in conversations. From year to year the stories become more numerous and, indeed, more fabulous. They will undoubtedly continue to do so for many years to come.

2 Text

"The culture of a people," writes Clifford Geertz in a well-known passage, "is an ensemble of texts, themselves ensembles, which the anthropologist strains to read over the shoulders of those to whom they properly belong" (1973, 452). This is an appealing image: like poems, myths or paintings so, too, events can be imagined as texts, that, when properly interpreted, provide cracks of illumination upon an entire cultural system. The task is both challenging and complicated. The argument is not that a single event or set of behaviors (like a bullfight in Spain or a cockfight in Bali) provides the "master text" for an entire culture: cultures are much too complex and contradictory to be properly reduced to a single stereotype. Nor is it claimed that there is a single correct interpretation or rendering of them. Yet certain events are so richly packed and glowing with meanings that unraveling them can provide new shades and levels of understanding.

Rabbi Chouri's *hillula* is such an event. It is a complex, many-sided festivity ("multivocal" it was said previously, "speaking with many voices") that both compresses and expresses a world of different cultural themes and symbols. Like other texts, it invites our reading "over the shoulders" of the participants.

This chapter mainly documents and depicts Rabbi Chouri's *hillula* as a cultural text, and those that follow present a number of different readings and interpretations of it. Three closely related questions are posed: What activities and behaviors take place during this pilgrimage? Who takes part in the festivities? And why do they come; what brings these celebrants to the cemetery?

We begin by examining the actual events of the day. Ever since the first small family gathering at the graveside in 1958 the *hillula* has gradually taken on a regular form. The different activities that together make up the substance of the celebration follow each other in what has become a traditional, expected rhythm: from year to year the pilgrimage unfolds in accordance with a certain pattern or script.

The date of the *hillula* is set according to the Hebrew calendar: Rabbi Chouri died on *kaf-heh b'Iyar*, or the twenty-fifth day of the month of Iyar, and the *hillula* is always celebrated on that date (unless it falls on a Sabbath, in which case it is usually advanced by a day).[1] Calculated in terms of the Roman calendar (the Hebrew calendar is lunar, and the date therefore changes from year to year) the pilgrimage takes place late in April or during May. This is the spring or early summer season in Beersheba, and it is not unusual for the celebration to take place under a blazing sun. As was noted, this time of the year is filled with holidays; for example, many of those who take part in the *hillula* in Beersheba previously attended the giant Lag b'Omer pilgrimage in Meron. This is, in short, a particularly festive time of the year.

Preparations for the *hillula* begin several months in advance of the pilgrimage itself. Members of the Chouri family and several of their Tunisian friends are involved in these activities. They spend many hours making preliminary arrangements. Some "improvements" may be made around the grave; modest decorations are added to the shrine, and fences or other barriers may be put up in order to better control the anticipated crowds. Over the years the grave itself has been covered with a metal cupola that provides shade during the day, and benches have also been installed alongside the *zaddik's* tombstone. Appropriate biblical verses are inscribed in large letters along each of the four sides of the metal covering. This decorative work is simple and dignified: even though the shrine is not set apart from the other graves these decorations succeed in marking it off and thereby provide it with a special character and distinction.

As the day of the *hillula* draws closer various announcements publicizing the event begin to appear. Posters announcing the *hillula* are printed and distributed throughout Beersheba and the nearby Negev towns and villages. They are simple in format: a logolike photograph of the rabbi appears at the top, and beneath it the poster states in large letters the date that the pilgrimage is to take place, notes that special bus service will be provided throughout the day between Beersheba's central bus depot and the cemetery, and invites everyone to attend. Letters and personal invitations are also sent to the rabbis and other leading members of the Tunisian community. In addition, the local newspapers carry articles about Rabbi Chouri's *hillula*, typically closing with the statement that "thousands of participants from all over Israel are expected to take part in the festivities."

Although practically all of the energy and activity is focused upon the day of the pilgrimage, the events connected with the celebration begin on the Sabbath that immediately precedes the *hillula*. Members of the Chouri family, their close friends, and guests gather together in a small neighborhood synagogue that bears Rabbi Chouri's name. Located off a plain Beersheba street, the synagogue was built in the early 1960s and maintains its bright, airy appearance. As has become common throughout Israel, membership in the Chouri synagogue has a practically exclusive ethnic basis—nearly all of those who regularly attend are Tunisian in origin. Attendance is particulary high and the mood especially festive on the Sabbath prior to the *hillula*; in addition to the regular Sabbath prayers several other psalms are specially recited in memory of the *zaddik*, and sermons and talks are also presented that recall Rabbi Chouri's memory. A well-known religious cantor may be invited to sing special melodies, and then, when the prayers have been concluded, members of the family and their many guests sit down together to a grand meal. The mood is happy, uplifting, in anticipation of the pilgrimage that will soon take place. This is a signal for the opening of the festivities: Rabbi Chouri's *hillula* is, in effect, about to begin.

The pattern of the day itself—or better still, its distinctive rhythm—is of great importance. Although there is neither a fixed time schedule nor a single central event around which the entire day is built, the flow of persons, their expectations, and behavior provide a tempo that moves and builds in a thoroughly naturalistic fashion. The thousands of participants take part, almost as actors, within an unfolding scenario of belief and act. These events were recorded in my field notes, and in the following sections they are brought together and related in detail.

8:30 A.M. When I arrived there already was a small crowd of persons clustered around the shrine. One of the Rabbi's sons, Yosef, stood at the head of the grave, busily pronouncing blessings upon those who stood before him, calling out to supplicants around the grave, and generally seeing to it that everything was in order. Several of his Tunisian friends from the synagogue stood nearby under the canopy; farther away, along a path between the graves leading to the shrine, another of the Chouri brothers had positioned himself behind a small table, and he greeted the pilgrims on their way to the Rabbi's grave. I walked over to Yosef, we shook hands, and he told me that he had been there since earlier in the morning, having arrived at 6:30 A.M. He was not the first, he said; a number of persons apparently had been there since dawn. As we chatted he continued to glance around, called out to several women to stay on the other side of the tomb, and, turning about, instructed them where to place their burning candles. The crowd was small and the mood relaxed.

The majority of those in the cemetery at this hour are women. They dominate the scene. The women seem to be of all ages — stout matriarchs in their sixties or seventies, but mainly younger matrons in their thirties or forties, with a sprinkling of even younger women as well. Nearly all of them are North African, meaning that they are either Tunisian or Moroccan. The women have their hair covered properly with a small cloth or shawl, and many wear large printed festive dresses. Now and again a more elegantly dressed woman appears, and occasionally one sees young girls dressed in their army uniforms. None of the women at this hour are in traditional costume. They seem to come to the *hillula* in small groups of three or four, although in some instances they are by themselves.

The women crowd around the grave — some place their hands directly upon the tomb, others break out in tears and then suddenly swoop down and prostrate themselves upon the gravestone, and still others sit quietly, apparently deep in thought or contemplation, on the bench further back. All of the time they recite or mumble prayers. Many of the women have brought some food with them, usually including packets of nuts, hard candies, and packaged cookies. They also bring small bottles or containers of a mixture of water and scent and, in some cases, olive oil. The women are kept on their side of the shrine, separated from the men. They have probably been to the *mikva*, or ritual bath, on the days preceding the *hillula*; menstruating woman are believed to be polluting, and ritual purification in the *mikva* is required so that they will not endanger or pollute the male pilgrims. The nuts and hard candies are also selected for this reason — they are believed to be "neutral foods" that do not transfer pollution.

Standing next to the elevated gravestone, the women place the food and liquids directly upon the grave: the food is thought to thereby absorb mystic, healing powers, and afterwards it is consumed, offered to others, or taken home. Some of them also pour oil or scented water upon the grave and then smear it over their face and body; this scent is also believed to have special powers. At this early hour a few have brought plates of couscous, and they eat a spoon or two of food while standing next to the grave and also offer the plate to others. Small beakers of arak are passed between the men and women, and everyone pronounces the blessing and drinks.

While they remain next to the grave many of the women ask that a prayer be recited for them. In some cases it is in memory of a deceased mother or father, and in others it is a prayer for good health or recovery from illness for a child or a relative. If there is a son or husband serving in the army the request is that "the Rabbi protect him from harm." From time to time a woman also appears carrying a small child; she may place the child bodily upon the grave and request that he or she be blessed and thereby, hopefully, cured. These children are seriously ill or have had accidents or birth defects, and the mothers have come to pray for the *zaddik*'s intervention. In all these instances the prayers are recited by one of the rabbi's sons or one of the Tunisian men helping them. They are pronounced rapidly and in a loud voice so that everyone can hear. The women then pass money to the rabbi's sons in return for the blessing: this exchange is done quickly, and if the sum is large the supplicant may ask for and receive a receipt (apparently this is kept for the Israeli tax authorities). The amounts of money are usually small, ranging from ten to twenty shekels (the equivalent of about seven to fourteen dollars), although at times they are much larger. The money is then placed inside a small wooden box that stands at the head of the grave. The rabbi's sons and others also sell packets of white string that have been blessed and small boxes of candles; the candles are almost immediately lit and consumed, while the string, which is thought to ward off illness and promote fertility, is later bound around the woman's hand or body.[2]

Since the crowds are still small at this hour the women may remain around the *zaddik*'s grave for five to ten minutes; many wish to stay longer, but Yosef and the other men scold them and insist that they move along and make room for others. Leaving the shrine, the women turn and place or toss the packages of candles into a large metal barrel standing nearby, where a fire burns throughout the day. These are memorial candles, dedicated to the memory of the dead, and they quickly disappear in the flames. After this the women divide into small groups and move away. They have brought baskets of food with them, and many sit on the ground or stand along one of the cemetery paths while eating their meal; the food is festive, and commonly includes couscous made with chicken or meat. Some of the women also pass through the crowd with platters of food and ask others to share a spoonful with them. When they have finished eating they gather together to chat, gossip, or join in singing traditional melodies. Clustered in small circles, sitting in the shade of trees or gravestones, some of the women remain for hours intermittently breaking out into lively songs. As the crowds grow larger they spread further away from the rabbi's tomb and spill over to the rows of graves in the distance.

At this hour of the morning men are definitely in the minority. There are a few older men or aged couples, but most of the men seem to be alone. They tend to be in their late forties, fifties or older, and almost all are Tunisian or Moroccan in origin. Some of the Tunisians are friends of the Chouri family who have come to help in organizing the *hillula*. They are all modestly dressed with white or colored shirts open at the neck, their heads covered with the traditional *kippah* (skullcap) or, in some instances, a deep-blue beret. Those who arrive early first recite the morning prayers. They then stand or sit next to Rabbi Chouri's grave on the side opposite the women. Some remain there for half an hour or more, deep in reflection or swaying slightly as they read the biblical psalms. The men also request that the rabbi's son recite a prayer for some loved one, and they light memorial candles and toss them into the nearby barrel. The men tend to be more composed than the women, and although they, too, linger near the shrine they later move away to eat, drink, and rest in the shade.

Near to the *zaddik's* grave, along the main path, a stout Moroccan lady has set up a rough table: she helps to dispense food and drink, and offers to wash the plates of those who have completed their meal. She tends the shrine throughout the year, making certain that it is clean and orderly. In fact, she is a kind of self-appointed keeper of Rabbi Chouri's grave and seems to be a rival of the rabbi's sons. She also sells lengths of magical white string, and from time to time, her face glowing, she throws back her head and shouts out tunes together with a small flock of women.

There are no more than from 300 to 400 persons present at this early morning hour. They remain close to the shrine itself, and while most of these pilgrims will remain in the cemetery throughout the day others leave for home an hour or two later. Several beggars arrive and take up a position along the path leading directly to the tomb: they are bearded ancients dressed in a frayed *jellaba*, a full-length cloak traditionally worn by North African men. Hawkers and peddlars also come and begin to set up their stands along the edges of the main paths. Some sell large framed pictures of Rabbi Chouri or of the Baba Sali, another famous new *zaddik*, others sell food and drink, a few display religious books, and still others arrive with supplies of cheap jewelry or trinkets. A small corps of Beersheba municipal wardens are also present, and with good humor they try to keep the sellers from spilling over onto the graves. The *hillula* has just begun: it is still cool and relatively quiet, with the activities concentrated around the rabbi's grave, but the anticipation is that the heat and the crowds will grow during the day.

2:30 P.M. The flow of new pilgrims continues, and the crowd now numbers from 3000 to 4000 persons. Some arrive from Beersheba by taxi, many others by regular or specially chartered buses, and still others by private car or truck. The police are busy directing traffic to a nearby field that has become a huge makeshift parking lot. Special city buses make the regular route bringing crowds of celebrants from the center of the city. Along the highway one also sees an occasional oldster hobbling along.

Those who come at this hour are usually in family groups— husband and wife often accompanied by their children. Some arrive in larger bunches of neighbors, friends or family members, and there are frequent cries of recognition and greeting as persons meet their friends along the way. In reply to questioning most identify themselves as being from Beersheba and the Negev area, but many others are from more distant places like Ramla, Lod, Haifa, and Eilat. They have come from all over Israel.

I strike up a conversation with several families that have just arrived. They are from Dimona, a town south of Beersheba, friends and relatives with their children, about twenty persons in all, the parents in their mid-forties and fifties. They immigrated from Morocco in the early 1950s, and they jokingly say that by this time they have become "veterans." Several of the men are storekeepers, another works in a factory, one of the women works in a nursery school and her friend is the secretary of an infirmary. They recall stories told by their parents about *zaddikim* and *hilluloth* in Morocco; they have been coming to this celebration for the past five or six years. Rabbi Chouri is famous and powerful, they agree; they meet many of their friends here and it seems to bring them good luck. No, they have never had a dream in which the *zaddik* appeared, but they tell about a woman they know in Dimona who had a chronically sick child, and how, after a dream in which Rabbi Chouri spoke and instructed her to come to the shrine and pray, the child became much better. They attend other *hilluloth* as well, although this year they were unable to take part in the pilgrimage to Meron. We drink some liquor together, the women begin to arrange the meal while the men go off in the direction of the shrine.

In common with this group, when they arrive at the cemetery each family looks for a spot where they can sit and eat their meal. The day is already hot, and they search for a shady place. A half-dozen or so set up tents in a large open area near the main entrance, but most seek shade beneath the cemetery trees. A few families may even use a gravestone as a kind of picnic table — they place their food and drink directly on the grave while eating a leisurely meal. The city wardens are there to maintain order, but no one directs or controls the celebrants as they spread out along the main cemetery paths. One section of the graveyard, a military cemetery where soldiers who died in Israel's wars are buried, is kept closed to the pilgrims; this special area is well-tended with clusters of flowers and a carpet of green grass, and during the *hillula* those who mistakenly wander in are told to leave. Otherwise, however, they move freely among the graves.

Before settling down the families first walk to Rabbi Chouri's tomb. By now the crowd there is packed tight and it may take as much as a quarter-hour of waiting before they can stand next to the grave itself. In contrast with the early morning hours there is now a roar of noise and built-up pressure around the grave. The pilgrims move slowly, wishing to savor the atmosphere, but are urged to move along more rapidly. During the early morning hours men and women were kept on opposite sides of the tomb, but as the crowd grows in size it becomes more difficult to maintain order and consequently both sexes are pushed or crushed next to each other. As they stand alongside the grave persons call out requests for a prayer or blessing to be said for the sick or the dead, and one of the rabbi's sons responds by reciting the blessing over the screeching microphone now being used. Sums of money are exchanged for the blessing, and the wooden box where the money is kept is periodically emptied. Some still try, without success, to place food or a bottle on the grave, but many do manage to drink some of the liquor that is passed around. The nearby barrel where the candles are thrown blazes and occasionally flares up with burning wax. The mixture of sound and smell is overwhelming: the crowd shouts out in Hebrew or Arabic dialect, the voice of one of the rabbi's sons is heard repeating prayers through the microphone, and the pungent aroma of burning wax and wafting arak hovers over the massed bodies.

When they leave Rabbi Chouri's grave some of the pilgrims turn to visit several other new holy places. Three other rabbis have been buried in the cemetery, and each of these graves has also taken on the appearance of a shrine: the graves are elevated and covered by a metal cupola, and around them a few dedicated activists stand ready to pronounce blessings, sell magical string and candles, as well as to relate the personal history and miraculous powers of the *zaddik* buried there. One of these rabbis is said to have been a pupil of Rabbi Chouri, a second is Moroccan in origin, and the third apparently is an American rabbi of European background. Two of them have their own *hilluloth*; these are small affairs mainly including family members and a handful of others. Throughout the day of Rabbi Chouri's celebration there is a continuous flow of persons to each of these graves: although the pilgrims pray there and some receive a blessing, these other shrines are not believed to be as powerful as that of Rabbi Chouri. They serve as a kind of "secondary site," other places that the pilgrims can briefly visit, and in this way they also reflect Rabbi Chouri's greater eminence.

Having stood before these shrines, recited a prayer, and perhaps received a blessing, the families return to picnic and eat their festive meal. Many have brought small braziers for grilling meat and proceed to cook steaks or kebab, a kind of spiced hamburger. The meal is eaten in a holiday fashion, each course interspersed with frequent cups of arak or brandy. Seated on a blanket among the graves, leaning sleepily to one side, the pilgrims often finish their meal and briefly nap. Among others the conversation grows increasingly more lively and animated — tales and gossip are told, those who are seated call out to friends who have just arrived, and some move from one picnic circle to another. Singing often follows, sometimes accompanied by the beat of a small drum: traditional refrains are also sung by the camped-out groups of women who, sitting together in the shade, periodically break out in a lively chorus. The songs are mainly Tunisian or Moroccan Jewish festival melodies sung in Judeo-Arabic; the tunes are well-known, and each core of singers is joined by others who form a circle around them and clap their hands with the beat of the song. Their faces shine, trancelike, with joy and pleasure.

As the crowd swells, the number of hawkers and their stands also increases. A small market begins to take shape along the main cemetery path. They tend to sell the same items—cold drinks, pictures of Rabbi Chouri, candies, and trinkets—but a few new arrivals sell watches, sandals, and gold-colored bands. Several ancient, saintly looking men dressed in a brown or white *jellaba* cry out that they will pronounce blessings; they place their hands on the forehead of those wishing to be blessed, pronounce a prayer and receive small sums in return. Tables and stands have also been set up in the parking lot at the entrance to the cemetery. Most of those gathered there represent various religious schools and charities. The young, bearded religious men stationed behind the tables shout out their message through a microphone, and this also adds to the general tumult. Prominent among these religious youths are those studying in the new religious academy named after Rabbi Chouri: they ask for contributions from those entering the cemetery, all the time noisily shaking their boxes filled with coins.

In the midst of this general excitement and pandemonium a funeral is about to take place. The mourners arrive, gather at the cemetery entrance, organize themselves around the grieving family, and then, led by a rabbi, walk slowly and solemnly through the crowd to the plot where the burial is to take place. Depending upon their own ethnic background, these mourners may be stunned by the sight of the cemetery transformed by the merriment of the *hillula*. In many cases (particularly when the mourners are of European origin) the pain and wonder of attending a funeral in the midst of this festive setting is plain to see, although among others (especially if they are Tunisians or Moroccans) there is a recognition of the mystic benefits of burial on the day of the rabbi's memorial celebration. The crowd quiets down, stills, as the procession of mourners quickly makes its way through the cemetery. But this quiet is only temporary, and once they have passed the hubbub begins anew.

The feeling of festivity grows throughout the afternoon. From time to time the regular beat of a drum announces that someone is dancing. The dancers usually are middle-aged women and an occasional man, although sometimes they include young teenaged girls. They rise to dance rather naturally from a group that has been sitting together, eating, drinking, and singing. The dance is Oriental (what in Israel is referred to as *rikudei beten*, a belly dance) and the dancers sway, move their hands and hips, all of the time taking care not to touch one another. A small crowd rushes over and the sense of excitement grows. It is a mixed emotion, though, since both the dancers and those who encircle them seem to feel that dancing in the cemetery may not entirely be in good taste. I listen as some in the crowd break away, complaining that it is not right; but others take issue with them and say, "What's wrong, we want to make the *zaddik* happy by singing and dancing." Suddenly a young woman forces herself into the circle of dancers and, verbally scolding them, succeeds in stopping the dance: "This is not a place for dancing; you're desecrating this holy day," she calls out. The dancers, who are slightly tipsy, glare at her and scream back in anger. She retreats, leaving the scene, and a few moments later the dancing begins again, stopping only when everyone, tired out, pauses to rest. I search her out afterwards and we talk briefly: she is a member of the Chouri family by marriage (her husband is a grandson of the rabbi), and dressed in Israeli modern-Orthodox costume, she complains about the rude way in which some of the celebrants behave.

6:00 P.M. The crowd is now enormous. What seems to be an endless stream of persons presses along the central cemetery path: they are mainly in family groups, persons of all ages, and while strolling along they pause to greet their friends. The men have come after work, and they are neatly dressed and relaxed; together with wife and children they search for an open space where they can eat their festive meal. The number of those grilling meat increases, and the smells and carnival spirit grows ever more enveloping. It is almost impossible now to pass in front of the rabbi's grave; the crowd is so large and intense that they seem to be carried along by the sheer pressure of the bodies. There are also a growing number of youngsters—teenagers, others slightly older in army uniform—who walk about in small groups as they scan the happy scene. There probably are between 20,000 and 25,000 persons in the cemetery.

The prevailing mood is one of happiness and satisfaction. Indeed, there seems to be a sense of pleasure that so many have come to the rabbi's *hillula* and that everything has gone so smoothly and well. The beggars and peddlers do a brisk business, and the young religious men raising money for their schools or charities continue to exhort the crowd to contribute funds. An hour or so earlier two well-known local rabbis of Tunisian origin (one of them is Rabbi Chouri's son-in-law) came to the festivities in order to help with the fundraising. They take up a position close to the shrine, and many crowd around them to shake their hands, call out a greeting, or chat briefly. Quietly and with dignity they suggest that money be donated for the new *yeshiva* that bears Rabbi Chouri's name. They remain for an hour or two, eyes beaming with good humor, and then disappear.

Two musicians have now arrived, and they begin slowly wending their way through the crowd. One is an older, slightly deaf man who plays a recorder, the other a short slim woman who beats a drum. They are well-known to many of the celebrants from their performances at weddings and other occasions, and as they pass through the crowds they are stopped by friends who ask them to play. They chat for a moment or two, someone offers them food and drink, and then the music begins. A circle is quickly formed, and everyone joins in the rhythmic clapping and singing. One of the women rises to dance and another joins her; then a young girl begins to dance, and the clapping grows even louder. The crowd swells—youngsters rush over to watch the dancers, and they clap hands and beam their approval. The merriment continues for ten or fifteen minutes, and then the dancers tire, the dance ends, and the crowd begins to dissolve. The men who had requested the musicians to play give them some money, and the musicians move off in seach of another group. The sound of music and song travels with them from one spot to the next.

The poster announcing the *hillula* states that the mayor of Beersheba and other dignitaries will make an appearance in the late afternoon. The mayor does not always arrive, however, nor are other Israeli politicians conspicuously present at these festivities. In 1981, when the *hillula* preceeded Israeli national elections by only a month, one well-known political candidate did make a brief appearance; accompanied by party supporters, the candidate wound through the crowds shaking hands, nodding at people, and engaging in occasional brief conversation. The response to this electioneering was generally good humored, even though some remarked that they were surprised to find politicians at the *hillula*. More recently a grandson of Rabbi Chouri has become actively involved in local politics. Elected to the Beersheba Municipal Council on a mainly North African religious party slate, he has also taken a more prominent part in the organization of Rabbi Chouri's *hillula*. Youthful, bearded, and filled with energy he spends the day close to the shrine, directing and helping the other members of the family.

The joyful spirit has now captured everyone: the crowds on all of the paths are thick and moving slowly. Persons stroll along, smiling at one another; some continue to exchange food and drink, others take time to visit the grave of a deceased friend or family member, those who have recently arrived stretch out on the ground, finish their meals, sing traditional melodies, or nap. A hawker selling huge balloons does a brisk business, and soon pink and blue balloons stretch high over the rows of graves. Around the shrine the Chouri brothers and their friends, fatigued but pleased, continue to pronounce blessings for those who have just arrived; and the crowd there seems even more tightly pressed together. Most of the women wear flowery dresses or skirts, although a few are dressed in traditional costume, adding to the festive air.

The evening draws close and, at first imperceptibly, the crowd begins to thin. The families assemble their picnic baskets, roll up their blankets, and make their way to the cemetery entrance where buses ferry them back to the city. The hundreds of cars and trucks parked along the road and the nearby field begin to fight their way through the traffic jams. As the crowd begins to stream out the peddlers make one last effort to sell their wares. Slowly, the cemetery begins to empty. The few families that have set up tents say that they will remain until the morning.

8:30 P.M. A small select group now gathers to eat the final festive meal. This *seudah* is held in the backyard of the modest Beersheba home where Rabbi Chouri lived out his last years, and where he died. Attendance is by invitation, and those who take part are all Tunisians associated with the Chouri family or prominent in communal affairs. Included in this group is a former government minister who lives in a nearby community. Tables and chairs have already been set up behind the house. The rabbis are seated at the head table, and facing them in five or six rows of tables, 60 or 70 men are gathered. Most of them have spent all or a large part of the day at the cemetery, and some, like the Chouri brothers, have fasted throughout the day. There is a sense of quiet pleasure, as well as weariness, about this assembled group.

The evening begins with several of the rabbis presenting homiletic talks. Their remarks are based upon biblical themes, and they are interspersed with references to Rabbi Chouri and the miracles and good deeds that he performed during his lifetime. The sermons are rambling and drawn out; the audience seems to be listening with only one ear, much of the time gossiping and exchanging remarks in Hebrew or Judeo-Arabic.

There are no women in this assembled group, and, in fact, a strict segregation of the sexes is maintained throughout the evening. The men grow restless as the talks continue: they yawn noticeably, glancing about, as nearly an hour passes. Finally, the sermons are concluded and the meal is then served. The food was previously prepared by the women, including Rabbi Chouri's wife, who have been working in a small kitchen for most of the day. The women—about a dozen in all—eat by themselves outside of the yard area; indeed, they never enter this area, and the meal is served to the men by other men. This meal, which includes several courses, is eaten quickly: the hour is late and everyone is tired. Members of the Chouri family seem exhausted. Following the meal the guests rise quickly, shake hands, and prepare to depart. Goodbyes are said all around, and the group breaks up. Some will board buses or private cars for a long ride home, while others walk or ride to their homes in Beersheba. The *hillula* has ended.

III

We turn now to examine this event. The seemingly chaotic, swirling scene that characterizes this *hillula* hardly seems to be an apt setting for conducting a sociological survey. How does one interview pilgrims about their age, present and past occupations, or their educational attainments? These are trivial matters against this setting of mass ecstasy. Besides, the crowd is enormous and the event itself is concentrated within a brief span of hours, and this poses limits for effective census taking. Nevertheless, it is possible to state some mainly impressionistic conclusions regarding who takes part in Rabbi Chouri's *hillula*.

To begin with, nearly all of the participants are North African Jews. Almost without exception those who take part in this pilgrimage were either born in North Africa and came to Israel as immigrants, or they are the second- or third-generation Israel-born offspring of Tunisian and Moroccan Jews. The exceptions are few and immediately noticeable. For example, during the morning hours several older European-born couples arrive to offer their prayers at the rabbi's grave; later in the morning they leave for their homes in the city. To cite another example, during the afternoon two stout Indian ladies dressed in traditional white saris can be seen slowly treading along the cemetery paths. When asked, both the Europeans and the Indian Jews reply that they attend the pilgrimage since they had heard from others about the *zaddik*'s miraculous powers, and that they have been coming each year to take part in the celebration. Standing out as they do in the sea of North African participants, these unusual pilgrims have a quaint, misplaced aura about them.

If those who attend are nearly all North Africans, then it needs also to be said that a minority are of Tunisian origin, while the majority are Moroccan Jews. This point was made previously. Although the *zaddik*, Rabbi Chouri, was from a Tunisian provenance, over the years the Moroccans have "adopted him": they perceive him to be an authentic, legitimate holy person in keeping with their own traditions. Moreover, since in Israel the Moroccans are numerically a much larger group than the Tunisians, they have become the largest and also the dominant group in this celebration. A rough estimate would be that only 15 to 20 percent of the participants are Tunisian Jews, while the rest are Moroccans.

Women certainly predominate during the morning hours and on into the early afternoon. As was emphasized in the previous section, the majority of participants at these times are women. However, as the day continues the sex ratio seems to become more nearly equal. Larger numbers of men appear after they have finished their daily work commitments, and they typically arrive together with their wives and children. Thus, at the least, both sexes are represented.

These features of social composition are more or less apparent and fairly estimated. Other aspects of the crowd's make-up are more difficult to assess with confidence. Take the matter of the ages of the participants: do they represent a kind of normal Israeli age pyramid, or are they drawn mainly from the older edges of the age distribution?

Certainly there would appear to be many more adults than young-sters; in this regard the normal Israeli age curve is reversed. Yet it would be wrong to claim or to suggest that the participants are ancients or belong to the 'older generation.' To be sure, most are adults, and a great many appear to be in the age range of, say, 40 to 60; but there are also a striking number of persons of both sexes who are younger, in their twenties and thirties. Particularly in the later afternoon and eve-ning the crowds of youngsters becomes more apparent.

This evident range in the age of the participants, whatever the exact proportions, is the significant point. Taking part in the *hillula* is not limited to or composed primarily of persons who grew up in Tunisia or Morocco, and who might still have vivid memories of *hilluloth* and *zaddikim* in Gabes or Fes. Many of the pilgrims are Israel-born or -reared, and their life experiences have primarily been within the Israeli, not the North African, cultural milieu.

The social-class membership of the participants is difficult to measure with any precision. On the one hand, the pilgrims do not appear to include many urban professionals, or more generally, the upper, affluent strata of the Israeli population. But then, Tunisian and Moroccan Jews are not strongly represented within the high-income ranges of Israeli society. On the other hand, there does seem to be a fair sprinkling of persons in the middle-income bracket. In response to questioning, some of the pilgrims described themselves occupationally as storekeepers, municipal and government officials, skilled industrial workers, members of farming villages, technicians at various levels, and the like. Many more appear to belong to somewhat lower social strata: artisans, small shopkeepers, pensioners, laborers and unskilled workers, low-level government employees, and others whose social sta-tus and incomes are comparatively modest. The socioeconomic com-position of the crowd is, then, a mixture of the lower and lower-middle ranges of Israeli society. Put in slightly different terms, this can be described as a "popular" outpouring of persons, popular in the sense that it includes and represents "the people."

The final point is to measure or somehow assess where the par-ticipants stand in regard to their religious orientation or ideology. Granted that pilgrims have, by definition, a religious sensibility, the question remains where to place them within the increasingly compli-cated spectrum of contemporary Israeli religious identification. In regard to religious self-definition, Israeli Jews range between "not religious" and "secular," on the one end, to "orthodox" or "*haredi*" (ultraorthodox) on the other, with a great many gradations in between (Deshen 1978; Leibman 1982). It is, of course, the "gradations" that make this system complicated. In discussion, many of the pilgrims identify themselves as "religious" (*dati*), and even more commonly as "traditional" (*masorati*). In keeping with these definitions, the men generally report that they attend the synagogue on the sabbath and during holidays, do not drive or travel on the sabbath, and women say that their home is *kosher*, or ritually pure, in regard to food prohibitions. These definitions place them somewhere in the middle of the religious spectrum – observant of religious traditions, but not overly zealous or entirely devoted to sacred ritual (Shokeid 1984). A few of the men do say that they are more observant, particularly those who have formal religious roles such as officers of a synagogue or employees of the government Ministry of Religion. The costume worn by many of the pilgrims also signifies their religious orientation: the small *kipah* or dark-blue beret worn by the men, and the flowered scarf covering the women's heads, are among the distinctive markers of "traditional Jews," persons who observe some if not all of the ritual commandments, and who also hold positive attitudes toward religious behavior and belief.

IV

Finally, why do they come? What impells or motivates these crowds of persons to take part in *Hillulat Ha'Rav* Chayim Chouri, Rabbi Chouri's memorial celebration?

The issues are, once again, complicated. The reasons for attending the pilgrimage undoubtedly vary among the participants, and they also are multiple and complex. Some of the motives may be clearly understood and easily formulated, whereas others are dimly recognized, if at all, and rarely verbalized. Indeed, in the chapters that follow several different interpretations of why people attend will be presented. At this point it is useful to examine the participants' own view of why they come to the pilgrimage. To be even more specific, it is important to understand the beliefs that compose so integral a feature of the *hillula*.

These beliefs center upon the *zaddik* and his power. The pilgrims believe that the rabbi, now dead, possesses magical or mystical powers and that taking part in the pilgrimage and prayer at his grave is both rewarding in itself and may also have certain beneficial consequences. That the *zaddik*, Rabbi Chouri, has great power and that he is able to perform miraculous acts is often stated by the pilgrims during the *hillula*. Standing close to the shrine, repeating prayers or being blessed by the rabbi's son or some other officiant, the pilgrims sense the shrine's powers: many stand or sit next to the grave in silent devotion, repeating to themselves thoughts or prayers directed to the *zaddik*, while others seem to be more emotionally excited, carried away by the ecstasy of the moment. They know about the rabbi's ability to heal and to help, and they have also heard of the miracles that he has performed in the past. This is one major reason why many come to the *hillula*: this day and occasion is a particularly propitious time to pray for the rabbi's guidance, and above all, for his intervention.

Those who cluster around the shrine have often come with specific prayers or requests in mind. These typically refer to a range of personal as well as family problems and quandaries: illness, female barrenness, the inability to resolve some vexing problem, or prayers for good luck in a new venture that the celebrant is about to begin. Such everyday, prosaic concerns are common themes in the prayers. What the pilgrims are asking in these messages is that Rabbi Chouri make use of his magical powers and intervene to bring about the desired result. A few appear to be tense, nervous, but most are relaxed, smiling: all have come to pray for the *zaddik's* help.

That Rabbi Chouri has the potential to influence the course of events is known from the many miracle stories told about him. There are a growing number of these stories, both collected in books and told verbally among the participants, that attest to his miraculous power.[3] These tales describe magical events that took place during the *zaddik's* lifetime in Tunisia and prior to his death and burial in Beersheba, as well as the many miracles that he has continued to perform since his death. His marvellous acts in the past are as important as those in the present: since he is now perceived to be a *zaddik* and consequently to have had great personal powers throughout his lifetime, the episodes from the past validate his continuing magical abilities. These stories—some tending to the mundane, others more fabulous—emphasize Rabbi Chouri's ability to see into the future, as well as his capacity to cure the ill and protect the Jewish community.

Three brief examples may help clarify the powers he is said to possess. One tale relates how, on the day that the rabbi was to leave from Gabes to Tunis on his journey to Israel, he became preoccupied with preparing his books and library for shipment and appeared to have lost track of the time. An assistant reminded him that their bus was due to leave Gabes at 2:40 in the afternoon, and that they would be late since it was already 2:00. "Have no fear," the Rabbi replied, "the car will not leave without us." And indeed, when they arrived later in the day they learned that the vehicle that left at 2:40 had a terrible accident, and Rabbi Chouri's party drove off several hours later. "I told you that they would not leave without us," the Rabbi said.

A second story depicts Rabbi Chouri's ability to cure illness. Once in Gabes an older man was suddenly seized by madness: he screamed endlessly, rushed about, refused to eat, and finally collapsed onto his bed. The doctors could not find a reason for the sickness or a way to cure the disease. The family then decided that the only alternative was to turn to Rabbi Chouri. They ran to the rabbi's home, explained the problem, and he immediately came with them. Entering the patient's home, the *zaddik* placed his hand upon the sufferer's head and pronounced a blessing: "It's hard to imagine, but just like a burning coal thrown into water, at that very instant the madness left him, and from that moment on he was entirely cured."

The third tale is even more eloquent and dramatic. It relates to the brief but tense period during the Second World War when German troops were stationed in Gabes. The Germans demanded jewels and gold from the Jews, and Rabbi Chouri, the chief rabbi, agreed to provide them with a substantial ransom. Soon thereafter, however, the Germans came with a different request: they demanded that within a week the rabbi supply them with Jewish maidens. Outraged, the rabbi refused. Throughout the week he remained alone in reflection and prayer. At the end of the week the Germans returned, and again the rabbi refused them. The soldiers left his home, but soon thereafter they seized several Jewish women and took them to their camp. Hearing of this, Rabbi Chouri locked himself into his room and prayed; only moments later the Jewish maidens returned, unharmed, to their homes. The women told how, on the way to the German camp, they suddenly saw two great lions stalking the streets. These were lions that the rabbi had miraculously caused to appear. Frightened by the apparition, the Germans fled and the young women were saved.

These miracle stories from the past strengthen the *zaddik*'s repute in the present: not only did he heal and bring comfort in previous years, these capacities have continued in the years following his death. Once again, they are described in a large number of tales that describe the wondrous saving acts that Rabbi Chouri performs in the present. The themes of these contemporary stories are similar to those that occurred in the past — they relate how the *zaddik* intervenes in solving personal and family problems, and also how he is able to resolve crises facing the community of Jews. However, the present-day stories differ in at least two ways. First, dreams are the typical vehicle of the contemporary miracles: someone who is ill or faces a personal crisis has a dream in which an aged, bearded rabbi appears and explains to the dreamer how his or her problem will be solved. Second, many of the contemporary miracle stories are told by and about specific living persons; a woman from Dimona, or a woman living at a certain address in Beersheba, tells how the rabbi appeared to her in a dream and how her problem was then resolved. The reality of these miraculous events are thereby grounded in particular living persons and places.

Barrenness is a common theme in many of the contemporary tales: in these stories a woman, who was unable to become pregnant and who for years had gone from one medical specialist to the next, becomes able to conceive after she prayed at the rabbi's grave or following a dream in which he mysteriously appeared. Other stories relate to healing: in one an aged rabbi who suffered from hiccups ("I could not pray, study or even sleep because of this") was suddenly cured after he prayed at the shrine and met a mysterious stranger with whom he left a bottle of arak. Another theme is how the *zaddik* brings good fortune. One tale describes how, following prayer at the rabbi's grave, a merchant was rather mysteriously able to acquire and then sell an old Moroccan bracelet, and how his commercial dealings subsequently prospered; a second describes a Beersheba policewoman called Esther Stern who had misplaced a packet of precious jewels that were in her trust, but who, following a dream in which an ancient holy person pointed to an envelope in her office ("Stop crying," he said, "they're in this envelope!") rushed back to her office to find them precisely as in the dream.

Miracle stories also center upon Rabbi Chouri and Israel's wars and dangers. One of these tells how during the Yom Kippur War an Israeli soldier became deathly ill after having drunk water from a poisoned well. He lay dying in the Beersheba hospital, and the doctor warned his parents that there was little hope of recovery. A friend then said, "Why are you waiting, go immediately to the cemetery and pray at Rabbi Chouri's grave." The father rushed to the cemetery, prayed for his son's recovery, and also placed a bottle of oil upon the *zaddik*'s grave; he returned to the hospital and proceeded to rub the oil over his son's body. "The doctors then came to examine him, and Dr. Lehman came out and told me that there had been a sudden turn for the better in my son's condition. After a few days he was able to leave the hospital, all because of Rabbi Chouri." In a different vein, another tale tells how during the Israeli invasion of Lebanon, several Israeli soldiers suddenly found themselves separated from their own forces and trapped by enemy troops. Worse still, their ammunition was almost gone and their position critical. At this moment they saw, as in a mist, the figure of an ancient holy man who appeared to be miraculously stopping the enemies' bullets while he led them to safety. It was Rabbi Chouri, and once again he had performed a great miracle.

In addition to wishing to pray to the *zaddik* at his shrine on the day of his memorial celebration, some of the pilgrims come to the cemetery because of a vow they had made previously. This is a second important feature of belief that brings celebrants to the *hillula*. In keeping with their faith in the rabbi's magical powers, these pilgrims relate that they come to the shrine because they had taken a vow to attend. *Na'adarti neder*, or "I took a vow," is how they explain the direct reason for taking part in the pilgrimage. This explanation is often offered by the women who cluster around the shrine, and some of the men also say that they took a vow to recite a prayer at the rabbi's grave on the anniversary of his death. These vows typically focus upon some incident that took place in the pilgrim's life in the recent past: they describe how they had been faced with some special problem or anxiety, and that they then took a vow to come to the *hillula* if their wish was fulfilled and the problem resolved. Putting it differently, they had prayed for the rabbi's intervention on their behalf and promised to come to the shrine if their wish was granted. In many instances these vows have to do with health and well-being. "My child was sick with a high fever, and I took a vow to come to the rabbi's grave if she recovered," or "My husband had been called into army reserve duty and I was worried about him; I took a vow to come to the *hillula* if he came home safely." Most of the vows are as simple and straightforward as these.

Dreaming is also a prevalent theme in taking vows. Women in particular report that in the midst of some family problem or crisis (a sick child, prolonged illness) they dreamed a dream in which the rabbi appeared to them and calmed their anxieties: "All will be well" he said in a caring tone. "After the dream things did become better, and I took a vow to come to the cemetery on the day of the rabbi's *hillula*."

The power of the shrine itself also attracts persons. This is given dramatic demonstration when, as we saw earlier, an obviously sick child is brought to the grave. Bundled in its mother's arms, the child is held over the tomb or placed directly upon the grave itself, while one of the rabbi's sons pronounces a blessing. This is an unusual sight — the crowds that press against the shrine mainly are not composed of persons suffering from physical deformities but rather those seeking to deal with life's problems. On the other hand, the belief is widely held that food and drink placed upon the grave does have special powers. Good health and good fortune are thought to flow from this food and drink: the oil or candies placed upon the grave are believed to absorb the power present at the shrine, and consequently eating them or rubbing the oil on the body will produce healing results.

As can readily be appreciated from these miracle stories and other descriptions, there is a profound belief in the *zaddik* and his continuing power to perform miraculous acts. There is considerably less of a consensus, or even a clear idea, of how Rabbi Chouri's magical powers are made effective. The pilgrims may have little doubt that this shrine is filled with potential power — but there is no theory or general understanding of how that power is released or controlled. Indeed, they seem to have little concern about these more "operational" aspects. What is significant is that the rabbi can perform these miracles. How this is accomplished does not seem to be of much interest. This is an important point, relating to the question of the *zaddik*'s relationship with God. Since, as the participants believe, God is the Almighty, what is the relationship between the *zaddik*, who although dead continues to perform miracles, and God himself? Here, too, there is little explicit concern and no formulated concept of how the *zaddikim* are related to God's powers. These theological points are simply ignored or not reflected upon.

Moreover, that the rabbi's sons tend the shrine and pronounce blessings upon the pilgrims, should not be interpreted to mean that they are thought to have special powers. This is emphatically not the case: although in this tradition a *zaddik*'s power can sometimes be passed on from father to son, in this particular instance the rabbi's sons make no claims to possessing saintly powers, nor do the pilgrims themselves believe that they are charismatic. Blessings at the graveside are spoken not only by the rabbi's sons but also by others who take part in organizing the *hillula*; it is an act of honor for them to recite blessings (just as it normally is in the synagogue during the daily prayers), but in no way is it seen as having a miraculous potential or quality. They are decent, dedicated, devout men — but not saintly.

Have all of the thousands of persons who crowd the cemetery come there to pray for the *zaddik*'s intervention? Can most or many of them be properly categorized as "pilgrims"? Many are, but others have come for different reasons. Attending the *hillula* in itself has a certain value. This point is subtle but no less relevant: participating in the pilgrimage has, as it were, certain immediate rewards and benefits. In addition to praying for the *zaddik*'s help, taking part in this joyful celebration is thought to enhance the participants' moral and spiritual qualities. This entails attending the celebration and while there performing or taking part in the proper rituals; what results is a heightened sense of spirituality and personal well-being, plus the promise of good fortune in the future.

Proper participation in the *hillula* requires performing a series of ritual acts: standing alongside of the *zaddik*'s grave and reciting a prayer, lighting candles in memory of the deceased and then tossing them into a burning barrel, eating and drinking, sharing food and drink with others, joining in song and for some, dance, and if one is a male, reciting the morning and evening prayers. There are even more specific requirements: the meal should include festive foods such as chicken and saffron-colored couscous, and women should be separated from men while they pray at the shrine. It is at this point that matters of belief enter again: the participants believe that if all of these injunctions are followed and the proper behaviors are performed, then their own personal well-being will prosper. To put it plainly, taking part in the *hillula* is widely believed to bring good luck, and this is an additional reason why many attend.

Finally, some go to the cemetery because the *hillula* is, or has become, a kind of attraction. This, too, is a relevant motivating feature. The *hillula* is a colorful, noisy, popular event, and this feature of the celebration undoubtedly brings many persons to take part. This is the day or the afternoon when "something is happening" in Beersheba of an unusual, grand sort; the cemetery is the "place to be" at this particular time, promising something out of the ordinary and thereby special and perhaps exciting. Besides, many of one's friends are also likely to be there, and seeing them in the crowd indicates that this in fact is the "place to be!" Many of the younger persons—teen-agers and older—who flock to the *hillula* seem to be attracted for these reasons, particularly those who come later in the day, and who then proceed to walk about for an hour or two. For them (and for others, also) the pilgrimage has become something of a "happening," albeit of a mystic, religious kind.

As the day progresses one occasionally can witness what seems to be a curious act: one or another of the male celebrants stands up and waves a large photograph of Rabbi Chouri high over his head. Waving the photo, exuberantly jumping up and down, he calls out in rising singsong tones, "*Harav* Chayim Chouri, *Harav* Chayim Chouri." This is a call of mystic joy. The pilgrim's sense of personal good feeling is so intense, his joy so powerful, that he literally feels compelled to jump in the air and call out. At moments such as these the photograph of the *zaddik* becomes an icon: spiritual powers are encapsulated within and emanate from this black-and-white old photo of the turbanned Rabbi Chouri. This icon symbolizes the meaning of the moment and, indeed, of the entire day. The pilgrims have been united with their rabbi. It is during moments such as these that the *hillula* truly becomes a wedding celebration.

3 Performance

I

If, as was argued in the last chapter, the yearly pilgrimage to Rabbi Chouri's grave can be thought of as a text, then the critical issue is how to understand and interpret it. Texts of whatever kind may be precious, but they need to be explained—"rendered comprehensible." As with paintings, novels, or symphonic works the problem becomes how to clarify this particular text's internal composition and dynamics as well as its symbolic meanings. Surely, there is no single "right" or "wrong" reading of the *hillula*, but rather a range of possible or probable interpretations, each of which should be measured by its power to illuminate and explain. Returning to Geertz's provocative image, we begin to read this text "over the shoulders" of those who take part in it.

This is never a simple task. Consider the difficulties posed in this particular instance. Rabbi Chouri's *hillula* seems to be a vast outpouring of persons all of whom are following different paths and contrasting rhythms. Families and small bunches of friends arrive at the cemetery from different places at various times, engage in somewhat different activities, and come and go according to their own individual desires or plans. As the day unfolds the crowds grow in size, spilling over from the shrine to the rows of graves nearby, until at its peak thousands of persons are packed densely along the cemetery paths. To be sure, nearly all of the participants perform many of the same ritual acts. Yet these are not done together or according to some grand overall schedule: each of the thousands of pilgrims seems to have his or her own particular pace and intentions. The scene at the cemetery is, therefore, characteristically open, diverse, and fragmented.

The problem should be clear: we need to discover whether some regularities or patterns can be found in the varied behavior taking place within this crowded cemetery space. Are there some ways to properly conceptualize the seemingly chaotic, uncoordinated activities that compose this event? More specifically what is the design, message, or meaning of the *hillula*?

One possibility is to conceive of the pilgrimage as if it were a performance. This will require an act of imagination, but it may prove rewarding. The dictionary defines performance rather felicitously as a "dramatic entertainment:" taking this direction, the point will be to conceptualize the events of the day in those terms, and thereby to see how the great crowds of pilgrims become actors playing a variety of different roles in an unfolding drama. In addition, we may also be able to see that, in common with other pilgrimages, this particular event both incorporates and expresses various liminal qualities. Throughout the performance a certain unfettering or loosening of social norms of conduct takes place, and for short moments of time different patterns of relationship become possible. The argument put forward is not that the *hillula*'s scenario is agreed upon mutually or followed equally by all of the actors, but rather that this is a contested performance during which several different, sometimes opposing, interpretations are advanced. These concepts—performance and liminality—as seen from a perspective emphasizing contest rather than consensus, will provide the core of this chapter's analysis.

As will shortly be seen in greater detail, these are closely related, interactive conceptual elements. This arises partially from the fact that performances of whatever kind frequently produce transitional or liminal phases of conduct. Like all celebrations, performances have the capacity to transform both their actual physical settings and those who take part in them. Beyond this is also a more personal element. Both concepts are prominently a part of the scholarly work of Victor Turner, and the fact that they are so closely related also derives from Turner's long-term interest in these topics (Turner 1967; 1969; 1984; 1985). To be sure, the analysis presented in this chapter parts company with Turner by adopting a more discord-oriented point-of-view. Nonetheless, the debt to Turner's work is clear: not only did he reintroduce the notion of liminality back into anthropology, as well as later playing the key role in pushing forward the blossoming field of "performance studies," in his later years Turner also carried out field research on pilgrimages in Israel (1985).

II

Performance has become a popular, frequently used term or concept in a wide range of different scholarly disciplines. The term is employed not only in theater or communications studies which is to be expected, but also in linguistics, folklore, sociology, social anthropology, and even history, which is less expected. What has made the term so attractive is the organized focus that it provides for analyzing the ways in which behavior develops within a set of frameworks. In one way or another depicting "a performance" draws attention to the ongoing process whereby certain actors "perform" acts of behavior in a more or less conscious, deliberate fashion, set within the broader framework of an interacting audience, an unfolding script or scripts, and a stage designed in a particular fashion. Performance places emphasis upon context as well as text. This can have the effect of practically reorienting a field of study; it is for this reason that Hymes writes about the "breakthrough into performance" in linguistics and folklore (1975), and Ben Amos and Goldstein propose that with a new emphasis upon performance folklore will include not only texts but also the "cognitive, expressive and behavioral dimensions" of how the texts are performed (1975).

The levels of abstraction as well as the focus of interest of scholars working in the different disciplines, or even within the same field, are expectedly different. This point is well made in MacAloon's introduction to a collection of studies that are all phrased in terms of the "performance genre" (the book is appropriately subtitled *Rehearsals towards a Theory of Cultural Performance*) (1984). For example, Goffman and other sociologists of everyday life make use of the term in their small-scale studies of interaction between egos and alters ("impression management" through performance) (1959); among linguists and anthropologists the term often refers to a specific ritual or ceremonial event (a Sinhalese healing ceremony) or to a public episode, such as the Charivari, an elaborate form of community social control periodically staged in seventeenth-century European cities (Kapferer 1983; Davis 1984). If nothing else, the range of different uses to which the term is put is certainly impressive.

When considered in relation to the *hillula*, all of these have some general applicability; there is a broad sense in which the activities that take place during this pilgrimage can be conceptualized in terms of interactional encounters, a performer's behavior, or a public episode. However, the most pertinent use is contained in Milton Singer's phrase *cultural performance*. Singer's conceptualization and the modest vocabulary of terms he proposed for analyzing ceremonial events, grew out of his and Robert Redfield's interest in the anthropological study of Great Traditions. More specifically, Singer developed and made use of the term in his studies of the traditions of Hindu civilization as these became manifest in the Indian town of Madras during the mid-1950s. His formulation is explicit and direct, and it is well worth quoting in detail:

> Since a tradition has a cultural content carried by specific cultural media as well as by human carriers, a description of the ways in which this content is organized and transmitted on particular occasions through specific media offers a particularization of the structure of tradition complementary to its social organization. These particular instances of cultural organization, e.g. weddings, temple festivals, recitations, plays, dances, musical concerts, etc., I have called "cultural performances." (1959)

Having identified and illustrated the term, Singer also went on to suggest some of the major features of these gatherings: "Each performance has a definitely limited time span, a beginning and an end, an organized program of activities, a set of performers, an audience, and a place and occasion of performance" (1959).

The recitations or Indian temple-dances that Singer studied seem to be of the same order of events as the festivities that make up Rabbi Chouri's *hillula*; or at least they can provide a starting point for analyzing the pilgrimage as a performance. Moreover, what takes place in the Beersheba cemetery can be thought of as including what Singer calls "an organized program of activities," "a set of performers" and an "audience." Other dimensions must be added — there may be more than a single agreed-upon script or scenario, for example, and attention also needs to be given to the ways in which performances are designed. Nonetheless, even though Singer's rather bare vocabularly requires both expansion and refinement, it has the advantage of providing a systematic way to begin the analysis.

This brings us to the second concept, liminality. The term is associated with the theories of Arnold Van Gennep, the folklorist who appears to have originally coined the term *rites of passage* (1911). According to Van Gennep, ritual events such as a circumcision ceremony or a temple pilgrimage could be divided into three broad temporal stages: separation, during which the initiates or participants were removed from their normal mundane pursuits; liminality, a "betwixt and between" condition brought about by highly charged activities, often while the participants were secluded in a special place; and reaggregation, or return to society, where they became reintegrated within their social systems, albeit in a different or redefined status.

Turner, who was attracted to the study of ritual behavior, took this modest formulation and rephrased it into a full-scaled theory. Initially focusing upon tribal societies and their ceremonies, Turner proposed a broad analytic distinction between a society in its "structural" as opposed to its "antistructural," or better, "communitas," phase: in the former social roles, relationships, norms, and sanctions were tightly ordered, whereas in the latter there was a "direct, immediate and total confrontation of human identities" and consequently many of the society's distinctions in status and power were reduced if not eliminated entirely (1969, 131). It was during this latter stage— "communitas"—that liminality flourished and, in fact, often blazed. Turner described these moments in the following tones:

> Liminality itself is a complex phase or condition. It is often the scene and time for the emergence of society's deepest values in the form of sacred dramas and objects. . . . But it may also be the venue and occasion for the most radical skepticism . . . about cherished values and rules. Ambiguity reigns. . . . (1984, 22)

Turner found liminality to be particularly powerful during public celebrations. At such moments

> The village greens or the squares of the city are not abandoned, but rather, ritually transformed. It is as though everything is switched into the subjunctive mood for a privileged period of time —the time, for example, of Mardi Gras or the Carnival Careme. . . . For a while most anything goes. . . . Yet there are some controls. . . . And ritual forms still constrain the order and often the style of ritual events. (1984, 21)

Turner's continuing interest in ritual and the sacred brought him to the study of pilgrimages; as he himself recognized, all of his previous work seemed to "converge in the pilgrimage process. . . . Pilgrimages are liminal phenomena" (1974, 166). Special emphasis was given to two phases of the entire venture: the pilgrims' journey, and their behavior once they had arrived at the sacred site. The journey—often long, tedious and dangerous—brought together diverse sets of believers, and traveling along the way they were said to experience a form of communitas: social leveling of past distinctions merged them into a new fraternity of traveler-pilgrims. Their experiences at the shrine itself were no less powerful, and there also antistructural elements broke through as liminality reigned; these were grand spectacles, emotionally charged moments of a high order, and previous social or cultural differences melted away as the pilgrims adopted universal symbols and new forms of behavior. A kind of Durkheimian concensus prevailed, even if it was profoundly different from their usual behavior "within society:" there might be personal ecstasies and unusual visions, yet at the shrine itself these highly individualistic experiences were patterned by mutually agreed-upon canons of conduct.

Turner's extensive writings on pilgrimage, as well as the universal model he proposed, have subsequently provoked additional research as well as considerable controversy. The field of "pilgrimage studies" has grown substantially since Turner's work was first published in the late 1960s and 1970s—detailed anthropological field studies of pilgrimages have recently been undertaken in Latin America, Europe, North America, India, Asia, and North Africa.[1] As might be expected, much of the controversy regarding Turner's model stems from the empirical findings themselves. To begin with, some studies show that modern pilgrimages are by no means lengthy, tedious journeys; modern-day pilgrims often travel swiftly by bus and train, and the epic Bunyan-like dimensions of the "pilgrim's progress" are largely absent from their experience. More important, recent research challenges Turner's emphasis upon communitas as the central feature of pilgrimage. These studies do not always record the merging of status differences between groups of pilgrims nor the refreshing sense of communality and equality as they stand or kneel before the sacred shrine; thus Eickelman, who studied a Moroccan pilgrimage center, writes that "the inequalities implicit in everyday social relations are preserved during the festival in Boujad" (1976, 173), and Sallnow, who did research on pilgrimages in the Peruvian Andes, argues that these events are too complex to be meaningfully understood by "the simple dichotomy between structure and communitas" (1981, 179).

The point is well taken: moving away from a "universal model" these studies may record pilgrimages' liminal moments, but they are also attentive to the flashes of discord as well as the rituals of consensus performed at sacred places. This perspective orients the analysis of Rabbi Chouri's *hillula*: not so much overt conflict but rather the pilgrimage as an arena where various persons and groups express contrasting views of themselves and the sacred.

III

Conceived then as a performance, Rabbi Chouri's *hillula* can be seen to develop in three consecutive acts. The first act consists of the small celebration that takes place at the Chouri synagogue on the sabbath preceding the *hillula*; the second act, which is the major expression of the entire performance, unfolds during the day of the pilgrimage itself and is situated in the Beersheba cemetery; and the final act is the *seuda*, the communal meal celebrated that evening in the yard behind Rabbi Chouri's old home. Each act is distinct and separate from the others: each is seen by the participants as a separate phase in the total performance, and each has its own special script, cast of performers and audience, as well as its own internal design. Nevertheless, although they are separated in time and space and seen to be different, they flow into each other in a coherent fashion and together compose the complete rendering of the performance. For this reason they should be considered as separate acts within a single "dramatic entertainment."

The first and third acts have much in common. Both are comparatively small-scaled — probably less than 100 persons take part in each, and they also are set within a small enclosed physical space (a synagogue in the first act, a backyard in the final act). There also are similarities in their scripts, or to follow Singer's phrasing, their "program of activities." Both are based upon and follow traditional religious scripts; in each of these acts a standard routine of events develops in a serial, unfolding fashion. For example, the morning prayers recited in the synagogue by the male participants, or the reading aloud of a portion of the Bible that follows, are parts of the standard sabbath script that is repeated each week in the year. In addition, all of the participants follow the same script at the same time — during the *seuda* everyone eats or recites a prayer at the same moment. Both of these acts are therefore closely coordinated internally and place emphasis upon the uniform participation of all those who are present.

Not only are there similarities in scripts, their stage design and composition are also similar. Common to both is the fact that there is little separation between "performers" and "audience"; to cite one example, at the *seuda* the rabbis, who are performers delivering sermons, are seated together at a separate table with the audience facing them, but they eat the same food as the others and mingle with them. This point should be emphasized — these are both intimate gatherings of family and close friends in which there are relatively few specialized "performer roles." Finally, not only are these acts small in scale, the same persons tend to take part in them: the participants at both the synagogue and the *seuda* are primarily members of the Chouri family, their long-time friends and comrades and a few others. Nearly all of them are Tunisian Jews: at both the beginning and end of the perform-ance the celebrants are persons who share a common background in Tunisian life and culture.

These two acts are comparatively minor. The pilgrimage enacted in the cemetery is certainly the main act, and it needs to be seen in all of its complexity and dramatic resonance.

Viewing this second act as a performance at first sight appears to be hopeless. There does not seem to be any shape or coherence to what takes place at the cemetery. Not only are there no main or "lead" parts, there seem to be hardly any parts at all! A single central focus is not immediately discernible—some of the participants light candles next to the shrine while others sing or nap on small patches of grass—and there is no obvious overall direction or order. Indeed, the immedi-ate observer-impression is one of chaos: hundreds and then thousands of persons pour onto the cemetery space, and each small group or individual behaves according to his or her own wishes of the moment. If this is a "performance," then it appears to be wildly erratic.

There is a sense in which this is an accurate conclusion. There are no "events of the day"—no large-scale activities or public rituals take place at this particular memorial celebration. The Chouri brothers and their close friends pronounce blessings next to the rabbi's grave, but these are by no means "lead parts"; in fact, their voices are practi-cally drowned out by the roar of the crowd pressing upon the grave. There is no fixed time schedule, and although many persons remain in the cemetery throughout the day there are no scheduled "happen-ings" or public occasions that they wait to take part in. As the crowds thicken, and some grill meat in the shadow of the tombstones while others pray as they pass next to the rabbi's grave, the conclusion of "chaos" would appear to ring true.

Upon reflection, however, *chaos* is not the correct term. It is not so much disorder as *spontaneity* that is being stressed and expressed. The sense or mood is not at all chaotic—there is no sensation of disar-ray or of nervous confusion and uncertainty. Rather, all of the partici-pants design their own time schedules and select from a range of

activities according to their personal feelings of the moment: spontaneity means that the pilgrims react directly and individually according
to their own moods and understandings. Their inner feelings or states
of mind are translated into behavior at specific moments deemed appropriate by each of them. What prevails is a sense of release, of having
become unfettered, indeed, of joy: this is the source of the excitement
that mounts during the afternoon as the crowd itself grows larger in size.
There are no hard and fast rules, except for the prescription to "behave
happily" on this day that memorializes the *zaddik*. Joy and spontaneity
are the correct terms as well as the appropriate ways to behave.

This does not mean that the participants act in ways that are
bizarre or unexpected. Quite to the contrary, their behavior is in keeping with quite usual, traditional practices. Prayer, visits, picnics, ululat-
ing, gossiping, and singing: these are among the traditional, acceptable
activities appropriate to a *hillula*. They are some of the things that
"one does" while taking part in a pilgrimage. The point being emphasized is that the particular activity one selects depends upon the mood
or whim of the moment, and since the crowd is enormous and each
makes his or her own choice, the participants engage in different "spontaneous" behavior throughout the day and evening.

Spontaneous, yes; but why a "performance"? In what sense
can these enthusiasts, marching to their own rhythms and seemingly
without a script, be thought of as actors and audience in a "cultural performance"?

Perceiving this act as a performance requires seeing the cemetery
stage at two different levels, or with two different types of focus. At
one level — in a close-up focus — what one sees are a great many celebrants organized into family or friendship groups of differing sizes, all
of whom are involved in the enactment of various rituals. The rituals
are by now familiar — prayer at the shrine itself, lighting candles in
memory of the dead, eating a festive meal, sharing food and drink
with others, singing, and for a few, dancing. This behavior constitutes
something like Singer's "program of activity" that takes place at cultural performances, even though it is in no way "organized" like the
Indian temple festivals that Singer had in mind. Instead, at the *hillula*
each of the participants enacts the ritual and performs as an actor — all
of the pilgrims have parts to play in performing a series of ritual acts.
Moreover, those who are actors at one moment, or in one group,
become the audience for others. This is especially evident when sing-

ing or dancing breaks out; many of the celebrants are attracted to the small groups of singers that spontaneously break into song, and the sounds of a drumbeat and chorus immediately attracts an audience that circles around the performers.

At this level, then, the perception is of a great number of separate small groups all of whom are taking part in the same rituals although at different times. In order to visualize the event more properly as a performance, it is only necessary to change the focus. In effect, it needs to be enlarged. Imagine now that all of these separate groups appear together on the same stage, all at the same moment engaging in different parts or phases of the *hillula* rituals. Imagine peering down at the cemetery and the celebrants from above, seeing (at this second level) how the various groups become linked and coordinated with one another. Perceived from this perspective the performance seems less haphazard; in fact, it begins to look remarkably organized. From this level, the performance state is better etched out, and the scenes or phases that compose it also become more evident.

The rabbi's tomb is certainly at "center stage." This is the main sacred space, and it attracts the attention of all the pilgrims; they pass in front of or alongside the grave, offer a prayer and are themselves blessed, light candles, and exchange food. The crowd around the grave grows and swells during the day until, late in the afternoon, the celebrants are literally carried along by the press of bodies that seems to be glued to this "center stage." Throughout the day they are conscious of the grave and the *zaddik* whose fame and power they are celebrating. The swirls of activity that rush through the crowd are always a kind of background to this central point.

The shrine anchors and orients the scenes that make up this second act: there is a continuous flow of persons within and then around this sacred space. With the *zaddik*'s grave as pivot, groups of pilgrim-actors arrive on stage and move toward the shrine, where they perform the traditional rituals. From this center they then fan out in various directions, at first covering the nearby graves and later reaching the trees in the distance, seeking to locate themselves in order to eat the required festive meal. At various moments throughout the day they then rise to greet friends, stroll through the cemetery visiting the graves of deceased family members and friends, join the circle of viewers around celebrants who sing and dance, or themselves break out into ecstatic behavior. Seen from this wider focus one feels the tempo of scores of new persons arriving, the crowd swelling in size until it reaches its collective crescendo late in the afternoon, occasional excited moments that are energized by song and dance, and then, as dusk approaches, the gradual exit from the cemetery area and the stage finally emptying. These scenes follow each other in regular order—the pageant unfolds with a certain timing and logic. What is more, this act concludes with a shared sense of happiness and fulfillment: the participants leave the stage pleased by their performance.

The design of this act includes a number of significant features. Openness, fluidity, and impulse are emphasized: the script being followed stresses personal choice in action rather than joint or uniform presentations. (This contrasts with the opening and concluding acts, when the actors follow a tighter script and tend to perform in unison.) In addition, there are only a small number of performers; the Chouri brothers and their helpers who pronounce blessings and keep order around the *zaddik*'s tomb, and the professional musicians as well as the occasional groups of singers and dancers can be identified as performers. According to the design of this particular event they do not follow a set program or overall script: each acts on a small section of the total stage, and the timing of their actions also are not formally coordinated.

Finally, no single person or group of persons imposes or controls this design. This is a critical point—no one sets this stage, arranges presentations, or organizes a sequence of activities. Rabbi Chouri's *hillula* does not follow a fixed time schedule nor is there a program of public happenings; there are few formal controls and little in the way of recognized authority. The design is essentially formless, emphasizing spontaneity and personal choice; this feature imbues the performance with its special qualities. As we will see, important aspects of the *hillula*'s message are expressed by its uniquely formless shape.

IV

This is one dimension of the *hillula* conceived of as a performance. There is, in addition, a second major feature of the day's activities—these are the liminal transitional phases that are, in effect, the consequence of participating in the performance. A number of striking transformations take place in the cemetery—as the crowds grow ever larger and the feeling of celebration intensifies, the scene at the cemetery takes on new and different features. For a time at least, liminality reigns.

The first of these transformations pertains to the quality and character of the participants social relationships. The *hillula* is a festive occasion—a wedding celebration—and consequently the prevailing mood is one of happiness and joy. Those who arrive early in the morning already wear smiles of pleasure and the sense of exhilaration and holiday expands throughout the day. Infused by this sense, social divisions or distinctions are broken down and feelings of communality grow.

This sensibility is given expression in a variety of ways. Strangers who come from different parts of the country meet at the *hillula* and exchange pleasantries and information. The groups that picnic together are composed of cores of close friends, but they also include others who are newly acquainted and have become attached to the group. Around the tomb itself the crowd includes some persons who are well-known for their public activities or wealth, as well as a great many others who come from modest backgrounds. There are those in the crowd who project the bearing of a patrician or religious sage, while others exhibit a more ordinary outward character. All of these persons are joined together as they share in the excitement of the rabbi's memorial celebration. This feeling is given dramatic expression by the tradition of sharing food and drink: women and men pass through the crowd carrying large platters of food, packages of cookies and nuts or bottles of arak, and they invite whomever they meet to share food and drink with them. The invitation is nearly always accepted—it would be rude to refuse this commensal offer, and hence spoons with couscous or cups of arak are passed from one to the next. These are signs of brotherhood, of the close links that bind all of those who have come to the *hillula*. The coins given to the beggars, or the money distributed that day to religious charities, can also be seen in the same light: helping, sharing, reducing inequalities is given repeated symbolic expression throughout the day.

A second aspect of this process is the extraordinary way in which the cemetery itself becomes transformed This is a central feature of the event, and it therefore requires special attention.

Under normal circumstances—that is, each day of the year with the exception of the twenty-fifth day of the Hebrew month of Iyar, the date of Rabbi Chouri's *hillula*—the Beersheba cemetery stands as a rather grim, unattractive location. There are both physical and cultural reasons for its forbidding character. The physical setting itself is stark and unattractive. The earth is hard, baked brown from the lack of rain; large portions of the cemetery area are filled with row upon row of graves and white monuments, while other parts are still bare, covered by dry grass and thistles, waiting for fresh graves. The military section of the cemetery is well tended, but the other areas are minimally maintained. There is certainly nothing grand about this place: the mood is somber. The cultural setting is equally unattractive. In Jewish religious tradition graveyards are dangerous places; the dead are polluting, and consequently priests, or *Kohanim*, are forbidden from entering the cemetery space, and those who do enter are enjoined to wash their hands less they pollute others after leaving (Feldman 1977). The traditions of Moroccan and Tunisian Jews are somewhat more relaxed. Generally speaking, graves and graveyards are not necessarily frightening or forbidding places for North African Jews; there certainly are potential dangers there, and yet in their tradition persons are generally more at ease while in the cemetery. Nonetheless, normal behavior there is typified by restraint and quiet. Funerals take place, bereaved families gather to bury loved ones and mourn their death, while on other cemetery sites families and friends assemble to quietly recall the memory of those who have died. These are highly codified moments in which all of the mourners have well-defined roles to play; indeed, it is partially due to the fact that behavior is prescribed that the mourners are able to contain their grief (friends gather close around the bereaved family, the eldest son recites the *kaddish* prayer, women cry loudly and burst into tears). A sense of restraint is characteristic of all of those who enter the cemetery: persons speak in low voices, if at all, and they stand somberly and rather stiffly before the graves of the dead.

How this contrasts with the *hillula*! The pilgrimage prescribes an entirely different set of behavior. Persons smile with good feeling as they enter the cemetery. Groups of women break into song, and there is a sense of joy, and at certain moments, ecstasy. Behavior is spontaneous rather than stiff and highly patterned; the participants drink and eat, shout out to one another, bargain with the vendors who crowd along the path. Families picnic and broil meat on open coals or lie down to rest next to the graves. Indeed, as we saw, some families picnic directly upon the gravestones, using the grave as a table and setting their food and plates directly on the tombs themselves. As the crowd grows in size the graves are covered, almost blanketed, by groups of revelers who eat and drink or pause to exchange greetings and sing.

The dancing and the circles of persons who encourage the dancers represent high points of contrast and transition: the dancers include both young and old, males and females, and they project an erotic image of gyrating figures urged on by the rhythmic clapping of hands.

In effect, the cemetery space thereby becomes entirely transformed: in the course of several hours what had been a solemn, restrained environment is re-created into a near carnival. The same space that had only a day or a week earlier been dry and unattractive — a graveyard! — is filled with energy and emotion. Behavior that would be outrageous under other circumstances suddenly becomes natural and normal: none of the pilgrims could imagine singing or eating in the cemetery on any other occasion. This is, of course, precisely the point — on the day of the *hillula*, this is no longer a graveyard but instead becomes a large crowded stage where a rollicking celebration is being held. This perception is uniformly shared by the participants; they all respond to this new environment. These changes are brought about not only by the massed presence of so many persons but, more important, by their exuberant behavior. To put it differently, the actors in this performance succeed in fashioning a new and different stage design.

V

Change, transformation, joyful release if not quite carnival — these are among the distinctive features of this particular performance. As the flow of spontaneity and the feeling of holiday mounts, individuals and groups play their various parts in the unfolding "dramatic entertainment." As perceived thus far, these are all tightly patterned activities — while differing substantially from behavior "within society," actions at this sacred space also appear to be highly conforming and consensual. Indeed, this depiction of the *hillula* confirms Turner's model of communitas in ways that are clear and obvious. However, there also are some more discordant notes, and they are no less interesting, relevant, and important.

The first of these has to do with relationships between the sexes. Jewish religious tradition prescribes different behavior for men and women. A fundamental feature of this differentiation holds that the sexes must not mix together in various activities, and in public places they need to maintain strict separation. This pattern is explicitly followed during ritual occasions; for example, within the synagogue men are always seated separately from women (women have no active roles in the synagogue, and frequently they do not attend), and only the men play parts during the ritual itself. This sexual division is based upon some basic features of Jewish religious tradition. Men are allocated the superior positions in all forms of endeavor, including ritual, while women are considered to be secondary if not inferior. In addition, sexual segregation is necessary in order to limit temptation (that is, women may attract a man's attention) and also since women are, or may be, in a polluted state: since menstruating women are considered to be polluting, men are enjoined not to touch them for fear that they themselves will inadvertently become affected.

These norms of conduct are well known to the participants. To be sure, the Moroccans and Tunisians who attend the *hillula* are by no means "strictly observant" in their religious outlook; as we saw in the last chapter, on the scale of Israeli religious identification most would consider themselves to be traditional rather than orthodox. The overall Israeli secular ambience has had a strong influence upon them, and many men and women move relatively freely together in public places. Nevertheless, the prescriptions regarding how one should act continue to be significant, and members of both sexes often strive to maintain the proper code of modest conduct.

The style and mode of interaction between the sexes while at the *hillula* differs markedly from traditional norms. During the performance relationships change and become considerably less encumbered. Women play principal parts during the day, particularly in the early morning hours: their more demonstrative behavior contrasts sharply with typical womens' behavior on other ritual occasions. Moreover, separation of the sexes breaks down almost entirely. This is especially evident among the crowds that form around Rabbi Chouri's tomb. Early in the day, while the number of pilgrims is still small, the rabbi's sons and their assistants attempt to form separate lines for men and women on opposite sides of the tomb. But even then, when the pressure is slight, this segregation breaks down. Later in the day, when the crowd grows enormous in size, men and women are pushed indiscriminately around the tomb: there are no longer two lines, but rather one huge crush of bodies pressing upon one another as they seek to pass next to the *zaddik's* grave. Under these circumstances members of both sexes inevitably touch or are pushed upon one another. This crowding and intermingling continues throughout the day as mixed groups stroll along the paths or as persons rush to form a closed circle around the dancers. In brief, as the performance continues certain normative patterns are set aside as men and women adopt novel forms of behaving.

Not only do they act differently, the women can also be seen to bicker and bargain with the men regarding how to behave. The relevant point is not only that new forms of action become possible in a situation defined as a *hillula*, but also that there are important differences of opinion between the actors themselves regarding what constitutes correct or proper behavior. This is given dramatic expression in several situations. Although both women and men cluster around the rabbi's grave, the men constantly seek to control the womens' actions—that is, they adopt a directing role in which they enjoin the women to stay apart from men, to say their prayers quickly and then move along, and they also become annoyed when the women place or pour food and drink on the shrine itself. Guardians of this sacred place, the men continually shout out at them, always wishing to control their behavior, preaching to their sense of proper modesty and correct decorum. ("Move along," "Make way for others," "Lady, why are you putting that bottle on the grave?") For their part the women struggle against these constraints—they are not interested in entering the "male space," but they are annoyed by the continuous barrage of male commands leveled at them. The women often turn a deaf ear to these orders and proceed at their own pace and according to their own practices: acting as if they neither heard nor understood these male commands, they continue to follow their own script. They linger around the shrine, take a step or two back and then return, stand deaf before the male shouts, or alternatively, carve out their own role by helping others and distributing food and drink.

There is a certain normative regularity to these squawking male and female figures jammed around the rabbi's tomb: the men delight in instructing and chastising the women regarding correct ritual behavior, and the women tend to feign ignorance or misunderstanding and then proceed to behave as they wish. This is a game in which all of the contestants are winners—while they issue commands the men confirm their own ritual expertise plus the fact that women are essentially ignorant, while the women prove once again that they are more clever than the men.

At various moments during the *hillula*-as-performance, men and women also separate themselves from one another. Men stand apart as a group when they pray together at the shrine: during the early morning hours a small group of men joins together to recite the morning prayers, and in the evening too they assemble in a male *minyan*, or assembly of at least ten men, in order to repeat the evening prayers. This fraternity of men is even more pronounced later in the evening (the final act) when the traditional *seuda* is celebrated at Rabbi Chouri's old home. This is an especially sacred occasion. The festive meal has an overlay of mystic meanings—many if not all of the men gathered there have fasted throughout the day, and the act of eating together on the date of the *zaddik*'s death is believed to mystically unite them with his soul. Women are barred from this occasion. Women prepare the meal, but they neither eat together with the men nor even enter into the space where the men are eating. The fact that women are excluded enhances the special nature of this moment—male exclusivity is a sign of its sacred character.

The separation of women is considerably more interesting. Singing provides the occasion when women are able to create their own private domain. Backed against a row of graves, sitting together in the shade, groups of women join together to sing traditional melodies; the words of these tunes are usually recitations of prayers, but from time to time they refer to contemporary places and events. The women have already eaten their meal and also drunk a cup or two of liquor and their chorus is vibrant and happy. The significant fact is that all of the singers are women—they become a sorority of enthusiasts who have joined together for some moments of merriment. Their breaking out into song quickly attracts the attention of others, and while they sing, the circle around them grows larger. However, men rarely if ever enter this circle: men stand or kneel on the outer fringe of listeners, but even when they are familiar with the words and melody they do not join this chorus.

This is a female preserve, a kind of closed section that is entirely their own—singing separates them from the men and establishes their own space and activity. What is more, this movement into song frees them from male direction and control; while sitting together in their small circles they succeed in establishing their own private world. Unlike their behavior around the shrine, the women are neither shy nor restrained: on the contrary, singing is the occasion for a certain strength and boldness of behavior. During these moments they are again following their own script, engaged in a scenario that sounds a mild note of discord.

These discordant notes grow even louder when dancing begins. However, what is being represented in dance is not so much the links between the sexes but rather the relationships between the Tunisian and Moroccan participants.

The issues are subtle, usually unspoken, and provocative. The situation is complicated: the saint is Tunisian, and yet the bulk of the celebrants are Moroccan. More to the point, the initiators, organizers, and "guardians" of this *hillula* are all Tunisians, while the Moroccans who attend in such large numbers are at best, guests, at worst, intruders. The Tunisians, who are the minority, have decidedly mixed feelings about the large numbers of Moroccans who flock to the cemetery. They are pleased by the fame brought by the large crowd, but at the same time they have serious doubts about some of the Moroccan participants' behavior. A certain tension exists between them: they too are following different scripts.

They are divided on a number of issues — whether to eat directly on the graves (the Tunisians oppose this, the Moroccans are indifferent), whether it is permitted to broil meat in the cemetery (the Tunisians would prefer not to, the Moroccans are again indifferent), as well as other matters of proper conduct. The critical issue, however, has been dancing: it is a kind of cultural litmus paper capable of distinguishing between members of these two different country-of-origin groups. The circles of dancers seem always to be composed of Moroccans, while those who are offended by what they consider to be inappropriate behavior and excessive gaiety are typically Tunisian in origin. The dancing is spontaneous — encouraged or pushed forward by others, a woman rises to dance, is joined a moment later by another woman, and then a man enters the small circle while one of the women retires to the side. Music blares from a tape deck or the musicians play their recorder and drum; the dancers stand and sway near one another, never touching, moving their shoulders and hips in a sensuous, rocking motion, with a frozen smile on their lips. They dance for various reasons — some simply enjoy dancing, for others it is a way of expressing their pleasure. Dancing also has its liminal appeal: it breaks a prohibition, but since the cemetery has been transformed by the *hillula* it is daring yet permissible behavior.

Dancing in the graveyard, with its attendant erotic connotations, has provoked recurring controversy. Several years ago a number of local rabbis — both Moroccan and Tunisian — publically criticized this celebration for being too unrestrained and licentious; they spoke out in particular against the dancing and also scolded persons for other excesses such as drinking and generally boisterous behavior. Despite this attempt to censure them, some of the participants reply that the *hillula* is meant to be a happy, joyful occasion, and they rise to dance again. As we saw in the previous chapter, debates and quarrels sometimes break out between a group of enthusiastic, slightly tipsy dancers (nearly always composed of Moroccans) and those persons who are offended by their behavior (usually Tunisians).

Some of the Tunisians consider the Moroccans to be too uninhibited; if it can be said, they find their behavior to be boorish and offensive. This is, after all, a Tunisian affair celebrating the *hillula* of *their* rabbi; *they* are the keepers of the shrine, and *they* pronounce blessings upon the crowds of Moroccans who attend. What can be done about "those persons" who persist in behaving differently? They glance for an instant at the offending Moroccans, then look the other way, shake their heads in wonder or sorrow, and exchange a nod or wink between themselves: and then, of course, at the end of the day, they form their own separate community. The concluding *seuda* celebrated at the old Chouri home is not just an exclusively male affair—the men are all Tunisians. The Moroccans are not invited, and consequently this occasion's purpose can be achieved. This is a small, intimate gathering, representing for the Tunisians the correct way to observe the *hillula*'s final act. No discordant notes are sounded there, just a quiet, relaxed gathering of persons who share their own understanding of how to behave during this exalted moment. In effect, they separate themselves from the others so that they may conclude the festivity in keeping with their own cultural tastes.[2]

If we return again to the idiom of performance, two separate choruses can be seen to be performing during the day. The Moroccan chorus is lively, demonstrative, and at times boisterous; it surges through the graveyard, frequently breaking into song and dance. In contrast, the Tunisian chorus is dour, solemn, and restrained, given more to prayer than to unrestrained cheer. These two choruses pass before one another, intermingle at times, but they never become truly merged: each follows a different scenario and consequently they remain separate and occasionally clash. Discord again breaks through: not communitas, but instead a contested cultural performance.[3]

The fact that there is no bedrock concensus should not be surprising. The theory proposing that ritual events are by their nature moments of high agreement where previous tensions and conflicts subside or are healed is obviously an overstatement. Why should ritual occasions—in this instance, a pilgrimage—differ from other social contexts where disagreements and competition thrive? To be sure, the *hillula* records many moments of liminality and accord, nor are the conflicts expressed there particularly powerful and fractious. Nevertheless, along several dimensions—gender and ethnicity—the lines of cleavage and contest can be observed. Sallnow's elegant conclusion to his study of Andean pilgrimages is equally applicable in the Beersheba cemetery: pilgrimages "are neither the sacralized correlates of structured social relations, whether political, jural, or economic, nor their dialectical antithesis, secular revolts manques" (1981, 179). The pilgrims bring to these events their own prior experience, sensibility, and self-interest, and consequently they are fields of discord as well as agreement.

VI

We return now, in conclusion, to the issues originally posed in this chapter: what is the meaning of this particular performance? What message is being transmitted by the thousands of pilgrims who yearly gather to celebrate Rabbi Chayim Chouri's *hillula*?

The pilgrimage is a "multivocal event," speaking on various levels and with several different voices. Not all of the voices have thus far been heard: a number of additional layers of meaning still need to be identified and explained. Nevertheless, some important dimensions have been presented, and it is appropriate to consider them in broad summary form.

Spontaneity, joy, and formlessness—these are the critical defining features of this performance. They enter into the activities in numerous ways. The pilgrims take an active, direct part in the celebration, they act personally and without reflection, thereby creating a mood of growing exuberance. This is a happy occasion, for some reaching to a pitch of ecstasy, and this brings about the dramatic transformation of the cemetery itself. There is also a minimum of organization, or practically none at all—the design of the *hillula* is expressed in the absence of a formal schedule or series of presentations.

Linking these three features together, what they represent is the almost total absence of hierarchy. Both the design and the "spirit" of the event downplay hierarchies. To be sure, the *zaddik* is and remains throughout at a higher level than all the others: his miraculous powers place him above the pilgrims. But everyone can pray and appeal directly to him, and none of the celebrants is believed to have greater influence or a more direct access to his mystical presence. Moreover, all those who come to the cemetery have parts to play, and they are of equal worth; there are no prayers, songs or other practices whose value or power is thought to be greater than others. There are different scripts, and they compete with each other, but none is deemed more important than the other: each is legitimate, and little in the way of censorship or external control is exercised in this nonhierarchical environment. Furthermore, no single individual or group dominates the event or issues commands and directives during the day: no stage is set where a few special performers make presentations, but instead the distinctions between "performer" and "audience" are minimal and keep changing throughout the day.

What this means is that the *zaddik* and his *hillula* belong to everyone. Surely this is one of the voices heard during these festivities. All of those who flock to the cemetery, ranging from members of the Chouri family and their close friends to others who come late in the day or for the first time, are able to become a part of this event. Everyone can find a place on this stage: the performance has room and roles for them all. The experience itself also is direct and personal, and this enhances the *hillula*'s attraction and power. The pilgrimage has an essentially raw, naive quality — the events of this day pour out in unchanneled form, quickly reaching and involving everyone who comes to take part. This adds to its strong sense of authenticity: there is throughout a feeling of genuineness, that this is a celebration that gives correct expression to the participants' sense of themselves.

Rabbi Chouri, the *zaddik* of Beersheba, belongs to everyone. Yet the two choruses — one composed of Tunisians, the other made up of Moroccans — retain their differences. The absence of hierarchy does not mean that everyone perceives this occasion or behaves in the same way; on the contrary, the *hillula*'s typically open design allows differences to coexist. This is best illustrated by the performance's three acts: the pilgrimage begins as an intimate, familylike Tunisian affair, then expands to include the many Moroccans who take part, and in its final act once again becomes a Tunisian event. Boundaries are drawn and then redrawn in this unfolding process. The interpretations also are different: the Moroccans perceive the *zaddik* to be their own, while the Tunisians, who *know* that he belongs to them, are prepared to welcome others to their celebration, but they also wish to maintain a certain exclusivity. While taking part in the *hillula* members of both groups are able to see themselves as both similar and different.

Finally, the message that rings out on this occasion is a celebration of the *zaddik* and his power. This is a festivity imbued with religious faith and belief in the course of which the pilgrims are expressing their understanding of life's forces and how they work. Their interpretation is founded in mysticism, focusing upon the saint, his shrine, and the miraculous acts that he performs. Not only is the cemetery transformed during this extraordinary occasion, the voices heard there carry the promise of good fortune and personal well-being. This is a hopeful message, an optimistic statement about the present and the future. This sensibility permeates the day—hope and belief in the mystical figure of the *zaddik*.

4 Process

I

Behavior can, as we have been suggesting, be interpreted in a variety of different ways. Rarely if ever do "the data speak for themselves" or with a single voice; if the truth be told, they do not speak at all. We explain events, render them comprehensible, by the questions we ask and the theories we construct.

Consider the *hillula*. Two themes have thus far been running through this analysis. One theme is historical, and it concentrates upon the unique chain of events that culminated in Rabbi Chayim Chouri becoming a *zaddik*. Following this theme has led, at the least, from Jerba to Beersheba, and it has involved not only the rabbi but also the thousands of pilgrims who join together in celebrating his magical powers. The second theme is avowedly both textual and contextual, and it focuses mainly upon the behavior that takes place in the cemetery; a text, the *hillula*, is performed there, and as the celebration progresses thousands of pilgrims play parts in an exuberant performance. Upon reflection, it should be clear that both of these themes are inward-looking, almost introspective in orientation. What they have in common is the attempt to interpret behavior in its own terms, or, putting it differently, to search out meaningful patterns within the events themselves. To be sure, this is one important dimension of the *hillula*, one voice sounded in this complex celebration. But there also are other meanings, other dimensions.

The *hillula* is by no means an isolated event. On the contrary, it is part of the overall experience of all those who participate in it. While at one level it may appear to be naive and spontaneous, at other levels this *hillula* is a resounding statement of major social trends. What this means is that the pilgrimage is closely connected with a variety of social and cultural processes taking place within contemporary Israeli society. It has not only an internal dynamic and message, this celebration (and others like it) is also a formidable occasion whose tones are loudly heard throughout the Israeli social system. Social stratification and inequality, immigration and ethnicity, the links between politics and culture—these are among the significant themes expressed during the pilgrimage to Rabbi Chouri's grave.

If the *hillula* is a statement of the life experience of those who take part in it, then surely it is a North African Jewish event. The point can be made even more emphatically: to say that it is intertwined with Israeli realities is also to say that it mirrors the continuing experience of North African Jews within Israeli society. After all, nearly all of the pilgrims—the 25,000 persons who each year join together in the Beersheba cemetery—are of Tunisian or Moroccan Jewish origin. Many immigrated to Israel within the last forty years, while the others are the second- or even the third-generation offspring of immigrants from these countries. While, as we saw previously, at certain moments during the *hillula* differences and tensions between members of these two groups become apparent, the participants all share a North African Jewish background.

The Israeli term for ethnic group is *edah*, and those who take part in this pilgrimage belong to either the Tunisian or the Moroccan *edah*; or, to use the broader category term that also is frequently employed, they are categorized as "North Africans" (*tz'fon africanim*). The conclusion to be drawn is clear: the pilgrimage to Rabbi Chouri's grave needs to be considered in the context of their immigration, initial entry and subsequent integration within Israeli society.

The definitive social history of North African Jewry, encompassing both their past in the Maghreb and their present in Israel (as well as in other countries), has yet to be written. At the same time, however, this topic has attracted the attention of a considerable number of social scientists and historians, and the scholarly literature on these communities is both comprehensive and impressive.[1] Some aspects of the immigration and settlement of North African Jews in Israel were depicted or alluded to in previous chapters, but it will be useful to briefly review this process now in greater detail.

Although small numbers of North African Jews immigrated to Israeli before 1948, the establishment of Israel set off what subsequently became a virtual mass transfer of population. Jews in ever-increasing numbers left their homes in Morocco, Tunisia, and to a lesser extent, Algeria, and in most cases their destination was Israel; at the same time a minority composed mainly of wealthier, urban-based elite families migrated to France, Canada, and several other Western countries.

Jewish emigration from the Maghreb was principally motivated by two factors. First, a kind of messianic fervor drew tens of thousands to leave for Israel, the old-new Jewish state; and second, the unsettled future brought about by the withdrawal of France from North Africa as well as the rapidly deteriorating Muslim-Jewish relations there led many to decide to leave. The immigration characteristically developed in several waves and ripples—a great initial movement to Israel in the period between 1948 and 1956, then a pause followed by smaller waves in the early and mid-1960s. In the process probably as many as two hundred thousand Jews left their old and newer North African homes. They were, to say the least, a heterogeneous, mixed group, including both a thin strata of French-speaking urban sophisticates from Casablanca and Tunis alongside so-called "cave-dwellers" from rural areas in Libya, plus, as well, tens of thousands of persons who had only recently moved to urban centers, together with equally large numbers who came directly to Israel from remote towns and small villages in the Moroccan Atlas Mountain region.

As numerous studies have shown, their Israeli experience during the first decade or two as immigrants was typically "bittersweet" and often plainly bitter.[2] In common with other immigrants then flocking to Israel—Jews from Romania, Yemen, India, Iraq, Poland, Turkey, Hungary, and Russia, to mention only a few—the North Africans needed to learn new occupations and skills, a new language and cultural styles, as well as adopt to what was for many a new, centralized type of Western political-administrative system. The immigrants' high hopes and optimistic dreams were frequently dashed by the harsh realities of Israeli life: they had come to a poor country struggling with severe military as well as economic problems, and they entered its social system at or near the bottom. In addition, many North Africans found themselves dispatched by government planners to new development towns and agricultural villages (moshavim) then being built in the outlying, peripheral parts of the country; new towns, such as Beth She'an and Kiryat Shmonah in the north or Dimona and Kiryat Gat in the south, were composed primarily of North African, and particulary Moroccan, immigrants. They were, in effect, "reluctant pioneers," only in small part understanding how and why they had come to live in these new, fragile and externally administered places.

These were difficult, often frustrating experiences, and the Moroccans in particular soon acquired a reputation for being hotheaded and aggressive. They were angered not only by the meager physical conditions of daily life, but also (and perhaps mainly) by the fact that the dominant social and political roles were monopolized by Ashkenazi Jews, the European-born Israelis, and their offspring and that they were expected to conform to the cultural norms espoused by this Israeli elite group. The pressures for cultural assimilation and divesting one's self of previous beliefs and practices were extremely powerful: a "Moroccan accent," or old country traditions, were looked down upon, and in common with other immigrants they were urged to abandon their diaspora past and "become Israelis." Then, too, the Moroccans sensed that discrimination and prejudice was being leveled against them (a study of a mixed housing-estate in the mid-1950s showed that Moroccans were the least well-liked group) and this, too, was a source of resentment.[3] Not surprisingly, the two major incidents of violence between Israeli Jews—the Wadi Salib rioting in 1958 and the Israeli Black Panther protests in the early 1970s—essentially involved Moroccan youngsters who were protesting violently against the reigning society and culture.

These were critical, formative features in the experience of many North African immigrants. But there were additional, equally important elements that became no less significant. Like other groups of newcomers they became loosely organized as an *edah*, or ethnic group, that periodically was mobilized and voiced collective concerns. Gradually, many of the immigrants began to master the new skills that had been thrust upon them; they became more fluent in Hebrew and at home in their new surroundings, and in common with other Israelis their living standards and consumption levels climbed steadily higher.[4] Now entrenched in large portions of the country they became the "veterans," instructing more recent immigrants (such as the Georgian Jews) into the mysteries of life in Israel. Even though memories of prejudice remained close to the surface, the newer generations of Israeli-born and educated youngsters were more confidently attached to their country. The Six-Day War probably marked a turning point: all segments of the Jewish population took part in what was seen as a triumphant national victory, and consequently they all became legitimately "Israelis." Furthermore, as additional evidence of their upwardly-mobile status, a growing number of Moroccan and Tunisian youngsters married members of other Jewish ethnic groups.[5]

In this heady new atmosphere the notion of ethnic pluralism began to replace *mizug ha'galuyoth,* or cultural assimilation, as the reigning Israeli cultural ideology. Jews from Middle Eastern countries in particular —Iraq, Iran, Yemen, Kurdistan, Turkey, Morocco, and Tunisia—began to publicly acknowledge and then to celebrate their different cultural backgrounds and traditions. For the first time the public schools began teaching the history and literature of the Jews of the East as well as the West. Something like ethnic pride replaced the previous self-hate. Not surprisingly, ethnic politics thrived in this new social climate. The successful rise of North African political leaders has been particularly striking; several North Africans now play major roles in Israeli national politics, and what is called the "North African caucus" in the Israeli Knesseth, or parliament, includes more than 20 (of a total of 120) Knesseth members who are themselves divided between different, competing political parties. The success of the North Africans in designing new national Israeli festivals has been equally impressive. In these and other ways Moroccan and Tunisian Jews have become more thoroughly integrated within Israeli society—they have, in fact, taken a lead in some of the transformations that have lately been taking place.

This brief summary does not adequately express the complicated path that North African Jews have been following. But it may suggest its uneven, bittersweet paradoxes. The issues can now be stated more clearly: how is the pilgrimage to the Beersheba cemetery connected with these broad-scaled social and cultural processes? What are the specifically ethnic dimensions of the *hillula*? And even more broadly, what is the meaning of the pilgrimage when viewed in the context of the unfolding North African Jewish experience within Israeli society?

II

These are challenging, lively issues, and they have been the subject of several previous books and articles. More specifically, a number of studies have advanced explanations of the revival of *hilluloth* and other celebrations within the framework of the immigration of North African Jews to Israel.

Some of the basic research on Jewish saints and *hilluloth,* both in Morocco and later in Israel, has been done by the Israeli folklorist Issachar Ben Ami. His book, *Folk Veneration of Saints among the Jews of Morocco* (1984), provides extensive documentation of the key role of the *zaddik* within Moroccan Jewish culture, and in a series of articles he has also described how new *zaddikim* (such as Rabbi Chouri) have been emerging in the new Israeli landscape. Ben Ami's analysis places special weight upon the North African, and specifically Moroccan, origins of saint veneration. What he convincingly demonstrates is that, in Morocco, saints and pilgrimages were powerful among both the Jewish minority and the Muslim majority. As noted in Chapter 1, hardly a Moroccan Jewish community, however tiny, did not have its own saint, and the two traditions were so intertwined that Arabs and Jews often claimed the same holy men and made pilgrimages to the same grave sites or other shrines (Ben Ami 1981; Voinot 1949). Ben Ami's studies show that *zaddikim* and *hilluloth* flourished among Moroccan Jews during the period of the French occupation, just as they had during previous centuries, and that new Jewish saints were created as late as 1944 (Ben Ami 1977, 171). With this near-massive historical documentation in hand, his conclusion seems inescapable: "the collective consciousness of Moroccan Jews with regard to their saints is unusual," he writes (1981, 283), or again, "the cult of the saints among Moroccan Jews had great importance and a central place in that community's cultural life" (1984, 150).

The thrust of these remarks should now be apparent: with *zaddikim* forming the focus of such a rich tradition of ceremonies and beliefs, it is hardly surprising that North African Jews should revive these customs in Israel. If new saints were continuously created in Morocco and Tunisia, how natural and fitting that this same process should continue in the particularly fertile soil of the Holy Land! When we narrow the focus to the *hillula* of Rabbi Chouri, the explanation of why thousands attend is relatively clear-cut: they pray and light candles at the rabbi's grave since these acts are a continuation of a powerful North African Jewish folk tradition.

This is, in fact, the explanation that Ben Ami puts forward in his study of new *hilluloth* in Israel; "one would not expect the veneration of saints to cease suddenly with the coming of most Moroccan Jews to Israel" is the way he put it (1981, 302). According to this theory there was an almost natural impulse to the process: transported to Israel where they became a vibrant ethnic group, it was to be expected that Moroccan Jews would revive some of their former traditions. To be sure, there were powerful pressures to give up the old-country practices — and yet certain key traditions persisted and, indeed, became further elaborated. In an interesting analysis Ben Ami outlines a broad three stage process at the end of which this particular custom was reestablished. At first, during the period of mass immigration from North Africa to Israel (the early 1950s), some North African Jews made trips to a number of already established shrines, such as the Cave of Elijah near Haifa. Later, in the second stage, modest-sized celebrations in memory of famous North African saints were held in private homes or in synagogues; on the eve of the *zaddik's* death a small band of the faithful organized traditional gatherings. Then, during the third, final stage (the mid-1960s) some new *hilluloth* began to take place "on a national scale, and to this people came from all over the country" (1981, 303). Rabbi Chouri's *hillula* is an example of this recent, third-level development. Another example is the striking participation of North African Jews in the yearly Lag b'Omer pilgrimage to Meron: whereas in the past this famous *hillula* mainly attracted orthodox Ashkenazi Jews, in recent years its size has grown enormously mainly as a result of the massive attendance of crowds of North African Jews (Shokeid 1974).

Ben Ami's point is well taken—it is perfectly plausible to maintain that the widespread participation of North African Jews in *hilluloth* derives from the persistence of their native Moroccan and Tunisian traditions. Emphasizing cultural continuities, especially with regard to religious beliefs and customs, is in keeping with a classical theoretical position, and it is supported as well by a great deal of empirical evidence: while economic and political modes of organization may change rapidly, especially during the upheavals of migration or immigration, religious beliefs and practices seem to be more resistant to change and therefore are retained.[6] At the same time, however, this is only a partial explanation, and consequently it is not entirely convincing.

Empirically, for this explanation to hold, we would expect that those taking part in the pilgrimage would belong to the older, North African born and bred immigrant generation. These older persons had previously participated in pilgrimages, and they would be expected to maintain the tradition. Yet, as was emphasized in the description of the *hillula* in Beersheba, the crowds of pilgrims include large numbers of younger persons and family groups who have only dim memories of Tunisia and Morocco, if at all. In fact, most of those who yearly take part in the *hillula* have lived in Israel for the past thirty years or more. This approach does not explain why they should choose to resurrect this particular tradition.

Furthermore, this interpretation is lacking on theoretical grounds. Since, after all, the immigrants brought with them a great many previous customs and practices, the real question is why certain traditions are maintained, while others are forgotten or recast entirely. The answers to these questions are to be found in the circumstances of the present, not the past: when considering why persons behave in a particular way (such as choosing to take part in a pilgrimage), it is reasonable to suppose that their choice of action is connected with or influenced by their current, present-day conditions and experiences. Following Gluckman (1940), who makes this argument as a kind of general axiom, as well as Yancey et al. (1976), who refer specifically to the behavior of members of ethnic groups, the point being emphasized is that behavior is best understood within the context of the here and now rather than as a result of memories of the past or previous practices. To be sure, this particular "cultural package," the *hillula*, is a traditional North African Jewish custom; but this hardly explains why it has been revived. Recast in this light, the problem can be formulated in the following way: what features of Israeli social and cultural life have led many North African Jews to take part in newly organized memorial celebrations?

This question has been taken up in an interesting way by Shlomo Deshen, the Israeli anthropologist who, among other things, first drew attention to the renaissance of these celebrations. Referring mainly to his studies of *hilluloth* organized by Tunisian immigrants who reside in a small Israeli town, Deshen observed that the participants included a large proportion of younger men (1974). The older men did not attend (the festivities were performed around a local synagogue), he explains, since they tend to be "purists" and worry that the ceremonies and the meals were not *kosher*, or ritually proper. But why are the younger men so prominent? For example, Deshen describes how a young man, clearly an enthusiast, shoves his way to the center of the performance, all the while not taking note of the fact that his *kipah*, the prescribed head covering, had fallen off as he jostled his way through the crowd. What is the source of this deep-felt devotion?

Deshen's explanation mainly follows psychosociological lines. The general background is the cultural crisis brought about by immigration from traditional religious communal life in Tunisia to the essentially secular Israeli society. This rapid transition, he argues, has produced a kind of identity crisis:

In the course of becoming immigrants their links to the tradition are weakened and these persons feel that they have lost their sense of self and self-esteem. Taking part in the *hillula* is one way of freeing one's self from this feeling of loss. This participation is concentrated, dramatic and emotion-filled. In their present circumstances it is much simpler for the immigrants to take part in the *hillulot* than to attempt to follow strict religious practices. The *hillulot* are a religious context that is especially suited to the needs and problems of persons who have lost a large measure of their traditional culture and social moorings (1974, 120).

Deshen's explantion is certainly located within the here and now of present-day Israel: persons are attracted to the *hilluloth* as part of their search for religious identity and affiliation as they experience the highly differentiated, mainly secular society of Israel. They choose to attend since it is one way for them to express their new *mesorati*, or traditional, form of religion. One need not entirely accept this psychosocial interpretation, and it may also be placed alongside of other explanations. What is important is the direction of the analysis.

This same general direction, albeit with a much different focus, is also taken in a recent article by Eyal Ben-Ari and Yoram Bilu (1987). Their point of departure is the fact that a number of new holy shrines have lately been created in Israeli development towns: as they correctly note, the process through which new "sacred space" has been established is concentrated within these small, outlying new towns. The authors go on to propose an intriguing explanation of why new saints and shrines have emerged specifically in these "planted communities."

Their theory is founded upon a certain contradiction inherent in the towns' urban development. On the one hand, these new communities located in Israel's northern and southern peripheries have generally suffered from an absence of sustained economic growth; throughout the 1950s and early 1960s they were characterized by high unemployment (or underemployment) and a constant turnover in population. Heavily dependent upon national government policies and bureaucratic agencies, they became "residual communities," "sinks" that became filled with the least enterprising of the immigrants who had been sent there. Indeed, "residents of development towns live in places . . . which are often viewed by Israelis with a mixture of condescension, mild disdain and paternalistic concern" (1987, 261). On the other hand, during the last two decades there has been a noticeable

awakening of local interest and activism, mainly centered around issues
of municipal government and politics. Moreover, to some extent the
population has become more stable, and increasingly is based upon
dense clusters composed of family members, kinsmen, and close friends,
many of whom have a real stake and interest in local matters.

Ben-Ari and Bilu conclude that the "sanctification of space" —
the creation of new shrines and saints — should be understood as a way
of resolving these two contradictory trends:

> The establishment of holy sites in Israel's development towns can
> now be more fully understood. . . . The juxtaposition of the "nega-
> tive" consequences of the earlier devices of planning and selective
> migration, and the "positive" outcomes of local activism and crea-
> tion of a sense of belonging created a dilemma for residents of
> many development towns. This dilemma — whether to leave or to
> stay and somehow change the town — was resolved for some people
> through the establishment of holy sites. (1987, 261-2)

In brief, according to this theory, *zaddikim* and their graves should be
interpreted as a "mechanism of urban transformation" (1987, 243). New
saints and shrines are part of a larger process in which the residents of
development towns attempt to explain or provide added meanings to
their lives: the new sacred space provides them with a deeper bond
to their community.

These two explanations emphasize different facets of the same
phenomenon: Deshen's article is addressed to the question of why
persons attend *hilluloth*, whereas Ben-Ari and Bilu are more interested
in explaining the emergence of new shrines and saints. The critical
point, however, is that both share an interest in interpreting these complicated processes within the contexts of contemporary Israeli society
and culture.

III

Taking these studies as a base and point of orientation, we can
move ahead to suggest a number of additional interpretations of the
hillula. These, too, place emphasis upon the Israeli dimensions of the
North African immigrants' lives, and seek to locate the meanings of
the event within this complex experience.

First of all, the *hillula* serves as one of the periodic occasions when
family members and friends who live in different parts of Israel can

come together and renew their former ties. The immigration from North Africa frequently dispersed members of the same family to different Israeli towns and regions; as happens so often in the upheavals of immigration and taking up a new life in a strange country, kinsmen and old friends found themselves settled in what seemed to be far distant locales. Like a marriage or a *bar mitzva* celebration, Rabbi Chouri's *hillula* provides a relaxed setting during which friends are again in touch with one another and where interpersonal links are reknit and information regarding one's social circle may be exchanged. This process can be observed throughout the day. As the crowd grows in size, persons suddenly recognize their friends and excitedly call out to them; they grasp hands, kiss, and happily exchange greetings in dialects of Tunisian or Moroccan Arabic. Friends and relations stand for a moment and chat, invite one another to join them for a drink and then settle back to exchange pleasantries and gossip. Some had visited with one another as recently as a week or two earlier during the giant *hillula* at Har Meron; they remind each other of their adventures there and laugh about incidents that took place during that day.

In these and other ways the *hillula* serves as a kind of "social switchboard" by means of which persons who live at a distance from one another are regularly connected and information is exchanged between them. These are, in fact, among the variety of motives that attracts persons to the pilgrimage. These reasons may sound considerably less dramatic than the mystical beliefs, or high peaks of religious enthusiasm, that were previously described. Nonetheless, they also help to explain why the *hillula* continues to bring together thousands of participants.

A second, related dimension of the celebration is the striking prominence of women. This point was made in the previous chapter: during the morning hours in particular the presence of women stands out, and throughout the day they continue to play active roles. This differs from Deshen's emphasis upon the participation of younger men —his analysis stresses the relevance of *hilluloth* for men in particular. In contrast, the social category that is prominent at this *hillula* are women in their late thirties and forties. This point requires amplification and explanation.

Most of the younger or middle-aged women who take part in the *hillula* are married and have children. In many instances they are housewives; home and family are their major interests, and throughout the year they tend to apply themselves to their household chores. There is, indeed, a rather traditional separation of roles between men and women, in which men are breadwinners and play the dominant parts in making family decisions and in public situations, while women care for home and family and tend to be less visible in public contexts. Women sometimes do play active roles in local neighborhood affairs, but the common division of responsibility between the sexes is one in which men are prominent and women remain in the background. Not only are these divisions sanctioned by Jewish and North African custom, in many ways they also have been reinforced by their experiences within Israeli society; even though equality of the sexes is ideologically promised and also partially realized in practice, women in Israel tend to be concentrated in certain limited spheres (family and home) and particular roles (assistance rather than direction) (Hazelton 1977; Shokeid 1971).

Women's behavior during the pilgrimage sharply contradicts these stereotypes. The women who take part in the festivities typically form small groups of celebrants; in some instances they arrive together as a unit, while in others they journey from different places and then join together at the cemetery. Like the male participants, they first pass before the tomb of the rabbi, recite prayers, and request to be blessed. As we saw previously, the women then move away to a shady spot where they eat and drink together, joke and gossip, and sing traditional melodies in a loud, vibrant, exclusively female chorus.

What characterizes these female groups are unusual combinations of joy and release, catharsis and aggressiveness, boldness and separation. For brief high-pitched moments the women are at "center stage," as others cluster around them listening to the tunes. This situation is unusual: since Judaism is a male-centered religious system, there are few regular occasions during which women do not remain on the outer edges. Participating in *hilluloth* is one such time, and events such as womens' parties at the *mikva*, or ritual bath, that precedes marriage ceremonies, is another.

The festivities taking place in the Beersheba cemetery can therefore be seen to provide the setting for a kind of female "role reversal:" women who throughout the year are housewives and behave modestly are here permitted to perform in a more assertive, boisterous public fashion. The *hillula* presents a diversion from their mundane daily chores; for a brief period they emerge from the background and act boldly and aggressively. Not only do these clusters of women resonate with power, their behavior is also deemed legitimate and proper on this particular occasion. Later, when they leave the cemetery in the evening, the women appear more relaxed, almost subdued: they melt away into the crowds, moving back to once again resume their regular household tasks. Whether their activities during the *hillula* are truly "cathartic" and thus function, as Gluckman has claimed, in such a way that they can subsequently return to playing their traditional subordinate roles, is certainly conjectural (Gluckman 1963). According to this theory their bold behavior frees them from the pent-up tensions and suppressed emotions that accumulate throughout the year, and hence they are able to return to their prior duties in a healthier frame of mind. Of course, the reverse process may just as well be taking place — these brief assertive performances may actually raise the level of female frustrations since the women return soon thereafter to playing their same previous domestic roles. Rather than being cathartic, the result may in fact be to increase the level of internal conflict. Which of these hypotheses is correct cannot be judged from the pilgrimage itself, and the conclusion must be left tentative and open. What is more certain, however, is that these female practices have become integral features of the *hillula*, and they provide part of the atmosphere of release that characterizes this celebration.

Although these social switchboard and emotional release functions are important, they are by no means the most significant themes being expressed during the pilgrimage. The vast congregation at the cemetery has considerably wider social and cultural meanings: more specifically, it should be understood within the general framework of ethnic group mobilization, inequality, and social stratification. This event is, or has become, what can properly be termed a *ceremony of ethnic renewal*. In this regard as in others, the *hillula* is not so naive a performance but instead literally bristles with social and political implications.

The term *ceremony of ethnic renewal* requires explanation. Festivals such as Rabbi Chouri's *hillula* — that is, festivities in which ethnic, cultural, religious, and political themes interact dynamically with one another — have been described in a wide range of different societies.[7] When chains of migration or immigration propel persons to different lands, and as they subsequently become organized in their new country as an ethnic group, cultural and political processes often intersect in the creation of new or newly revived communal celebrations. Typically these are public occasions during which members of a particular country or place-of-origin group join together to conduct joint activities that celebrate and glorify their past and present. The rituals that compose these events are performed by members of the ethnic group, while their audience is made up of other ethnics as well as viewers drawn from the society at large. Festivals or festivities such as these can be thought of as ceremonies of ethnic renewal. They take the form of parades, carnivals, street celebrations, festivals of folk art, religious processions, athletic contests, as well as various other formats. The cultural idioms infusing these festivities are usually national and religious—they include songs and prayers in the native language, artistic presentations of various kinds, nationalistic speeches or presentations where the flag and other symbols are displayed prominently, theatrical pageants where epic events are recounted, displays of native costume and food, games and recreational contests. What makes them ceremonies of renewal is that among the assumed or stated objectives of the festivity is the mobilizing, strengthening, and continuation of the collectivity; occasions such as these are meant to bind strong links between the group members, renew associations between leaders and followers, as well as present an overt demonstration of the continuing power of the group's traditions, both religious and secular. What is involved in dancing in native costume or singing the songs of one's former land is therefore not so much "folklore," but rather a statement of communal interests and power. These ceremonial occasions are, in other words, cultural and political events par excellence.

It can readily be seen that Rabbi Chouri's *hillula* is a demonstration of this kind. Participation in the pilgrimage has grown enormously; in a brief period of years what had been a small family gathering has become a grand, massive event. This in itself is important—the joining together of thousands of persons, and their taking part in the unfolding performance, gives the participants a sense of power and significance. In the late afternoon, when the crowd surges around the rabbi's tomb and practically blankets the cemetery area, the feeling of collective strength is particularly striking. This is more than a social switchboard where friends can find one another—there is a kind of elation, a Durkheimian elan vital, that is created by their packed, buoyant presence. No less important, the huge crowd is composed entirely of celebrants who are Tunisian and Moroccan in origin: the point is not only that this massive outpouring of persons lends them a sense of power, but that, in addition, they all belong to the same social category. Journeying to the cemetery and taking part in the *hillula* is a direct, personal affirmation of belonging to an Israeli ethnic group. The thousands of persons who attend are, in effect, demonstrating their ethnic identity and sense of group membership. If power is being expressed, then surely this is a dramatic manifestation of present-day Moroccan and Tunisian ethnic organization and strength. Not only is this *hillula* a North African event, it is also an expression of this group's heightened sense of its own presence and power within Israeli society.

Indeed, the feeling of being a part of a large and lively group of persons, all of whom share many experiences, beliefs, and traditions, is repeatedly given vivid expression. Eating the same foods, pronouncing prayers and songs in the same intonations, conversing in native idioms and language, following a commonly understood, well-known set of rituals — all of this has the effect of enhancing the emotional and symbolic links between the participants. Implicitly, all of those who take part are being reminded of their common origins, and what is more, their likely common fate and future. In contrast with other public occasions in Israel, no speeches are delivered regarding the group's past glories and present-day successes; no speeches of any kind are given since, as we have seen, this *hillula* proceeds without a program of activities or performance of public rituals. Still, the implicitly communal feelings are strongly felt by the thousands who attend. By participating in the pilgrimage these Moroccan and Tunisian immigrants and children of immigrants are symbolically defining themselves — they are marking themselves off as a group in contrast with other Israelis. In other words, Rabbi Chouri's *hillula* has the quality of enhancing ethnic group solidarity and affiliation and drawing a boundary of positive affect around the North African participants.

Beyond solidarity, however, are even stronger ethnic tones to this event. What attracts thousands of Moroccan and Tunisian Israelis to this *hillula* is that it is an occasion for them to publically celebrate *on their own terms*: this is "their holiday" commemorating "their rabbi" and it is performed in a grand style according to "their own traditions." This is a powerful message: it is now proper for them, Israelis all, to come together and publically celebrate the anniversary of the death of a Tunisian *zaddik*. They join one another normally and proudly with no hint of crisis in their social or cultural identity. There is nothing hidden, not a breath of anything unusual or bizarre, as they come together and fill the municipal cemetery. Other Israelis who happen to be there — mourners who have come to take part in a funeral or those driving past in their cars on the nearby main road — may be shocked to see how the cemetery has been transformed. But the Moroccan and Tunisian participants never apologize about eating meals or singing songs in the cemetery. They do not choose to explain themselves to others, they simply act in accordance with their own traditions.

How different this is from the recent past! As we know, during the first two decades following Israel's creation attempts to organize along specifically ethnic lines were frowned upon and discredited. All of the immigrants then pouring into the country were urged to give up their diaspora past and "become Israelis." Moroccan Jews were often the particular butt of social stigma, and as a result some of them sought to escape from their low-status identity ("I'm from the south of France, not from Morocco," is the punch line of an old Israeli joke about Moroccan youngsters wishing to flee from their true origins). The *hillula's* message is, of course, totally different: during this particular event the crowds that assemble are loudly announcing that they are North Africans. While they light candles and pray at the shrine or receive a blessing and join in song, they are proclaiming their ethnic identities both to themselves and to others. In addition, they are also demonstrating the fact that both as individuals and as members of their North African *edah* they are a legitimate component of the Israeli fabric. This is a dramatic statement of change — it is an indication that "ethnic pluralism" has replaced "social assimilation" as the dominant Israeli social ideology. In keeping with this outlook ethnic celebrations such as this are presently considered to be both proper and enriching: *hilluloth* and *zaddikim* can now be seen as North African "cultural contributions" that bolster the society's spiritual diversity and strength.

Finally, not only is this a statement of new-found ethnic power and pride, the message also includes an edge of resentment against the Ashkenazim, the European-origin Israelis who previously monopolized the society's elite positions. The memories of past times — only yesterday! — when the Ashkenazim looked down upon the Moroccans, are still sore and fresh. Sensing their own strength, the North Africans seem to almost dare the Ashkenazim to criticize them for the way they behave, or try to once again instruct them regarding what is right and wrong. It is as if they are looking for the opportunity to finally set things straight. This is a cry against the Israeli establishment, and what is more, an announcement that these former newcomers have now arrived and that they, too, are proper Israelis.

Taken together, these developments represent a true seachange, even though they are the result of many gradual steps. Moreover, these trends need to be understood in relation to the North African participants' rapidly evolving experiences within Israeli society. Looking back, they can recall those initial trying years when they were essentially déclassé, thrust into outlying places where they were expected to somehow build a new life; at the same time, they can proudly claim to have become accustomed to their new Israeli environment and, for many, to have steadily moved upward in the sociopolitical system. Indeed, the process of increased integration helps to explain why *hilluloth* have in recent years attracted wider audiences. It will be recalled that according to Ben Ami's three-stage progression Moroccan immigrants at first (during the 1950s and early 1960s) attended religious shrines and small-scaled *hilluloth* in modest numbers, while the great upsurge in the popularity of these celebrations has been more recent. This is the obverse side to social mobility and greater social integration: as these immigrants became more accustomed to living in Israel and more adept at moving upward in the society, they also gained the confidence and strength enabling them to begin organizing their own public festivals. The recent emergence in Israel of ethnic events is therefore not a sign of the failure to assimilate but quite the reverse: celebrations such as Rabbi Chouri's *hillula* are legitimate since the participants have become more thoroughly absorbed within their new milieu. These public manifestations of ethnicity are, in effect, symbols of their having become "more Israeli" (Weingrod 1979). Paradoxically, the message being sent from the cemetery is an expression of the participants' enhanced social integration rather than a statement of schism or deep division.

This is, then, a ceremony of ethnic renewal: the *hillula*'s specifically ethnic tones are loud and powerful. By taking part in this festivity the North African pilgrims affirm and rekindle their ethnic identities. The pilgrimage is not just a statement of mystical belief, it is at the same time an occasion for ethnic group mobilization.

IV

Rabbi Chouri's memorial celebration is also, at still another level, a decidedly political event. Or, to be more precise, it is a large-size

gathering that expresses a variety of political meanings and implications. Some aspects of this additional "voice" are clear and obvious,
while others are less apparent although by no means less significant.
Indeed, the most interesting political dimensions are more masked
and immanent.

This *hillula* is not at all what is usually thought of as a political
rally or a political meeting. Even though thousands of persons are
attracted to the yearly celebration, less than a handful of politicians
tend to be present at the cemetery. This point was alluded to previously:
although the placards announcing the event state that the mayor of
Beersheba and other local dignitaries will take part, they do not always
make an appearance, and even when the mayor arrives he and his
small entourage usually walk briefly among the pilgrims. In the past,
when the date of the *hillula* fell close to Israeli national elections, a few
national-level candidates might appear, but as we also saw their electioneering activities were limited to a rapid march though the cemetery.
In keeping with its unorganized, formless design, the *hillula* has not
become a platform for direct political activities or partisan party interests.

This has been the rule; however, as with all rules, there are several interesting exceptions. The first of these is a well-known political
figure who regularly takes part in the pilgrimage. During the 1960s
and 1970s he was a prominent member of the then-dominant Israeli
Labor party, later he switched membership and became a leader of a
small, predominantly North African political party. A resident of the
Beersheba area and himself a Tunisian, he has regularly attended the
hillula since its inception in the late 1950s. His presence is low-keyed
and dignified — he strolls quietly through the cemetery without actively
seeking to call attention to himself, and later in the evening he joins
his fellow Tunisians at the concluding festive meal. The second exception is one of the *zaddik*'s grandsons. A number of years ago he was
elected to the Beersheba Municipal Council, where he quickly gained
a reputation as an activist critic of the mayor and his administration.
Politically, the young Chouri represents a new orthodox religious political party that draws support mainly from North African voters. He has
lately taken a more active role in the *hillula*, and throughout the day
he can be seen busily greeting people and directing affairs around the
zaddik's grave. Like the other Tunisian politician, his activities carry no
direct or obvious political party label: as a descendant of the saint and
a well-known local personality he plays his role with forceful dignity.

The conclusion to be drawn from these remarks should be clear: even though a few political figures are present at the *hillula*, they do not attempt to turn this event into a political demonstration. This is, in a way, surprising: given the size of the crowd it is remarkable that many more Israeli politicians do not attend, and that active politicking does not take place. This is especially the case since party politics in Israel are intertwined with practically all public occasions; there is hardly an event of any size that is not, in one way or another, connected with a political party or political interests. In this instance, however, the spirit of the *hillula* seems to have inhibited any attempt to transform it into a political gathering. This mystical occasion celebrating the *zaddik*, set within the awesome confines of a cemetery, is perceived as an inappropriate time and place for such mundane behavior as distributing political party propaganda or attempting to generate support for a particular party or candidate. It would simply not be fitting or proper conduct, too profane to be readily incorporated within this spiritual occasion.

This does not mean that the pilgrimage is a nonpolitical event: on the contrary, this large gathering is rich with political significance. In fact, the *hillula* touches upon several of the major issues that both confront and confound contemporary Israeli politics.

The first of these has to do with the relationships between ethnicity and politics. During the first several decades following its establishment, Israel's political elites were practically all European-born or -bred Ashkenazim. More recently, however, the upper echelons of political power have included a broader representation of persons from Middle Eastern countries such as Iraq, Yemen, Iran, and Morocco. The prevalence of Moroccan political figures has already been pointed out; in the past decade in particular Moroccan politicians have had striking success at both the local and national levels. They are counted among the leading members of the two major Israeli political parties, Labor and Likud, and as we have also noted several minor parties have had a largely North African composition and political appeal. For a variety of reasons the Likud in particular has been successful in attracting the support of many North African voters. While these party leaders and activists do not draw all of their support from the North African segment of the Israeli population, there can be little doubt that North African voters often support North African candidates and parties. Ethnic appeals and voting patterns are, in other words, very much a part of present-day Israeli political realities.[8]

In this regard Rabbi Chouri's *hillula*, as well as other Israeli ethnic renewal ceremonies, can be seen to have political significance. The pilgrimage to the *zaddik*'s grave is one of the contexts in which North African identity and group sentiment is made manifest; gathering together to pray and sing songs has the effect of magnifying ethnic solidarity. The sense of group power that grows at these events can then be channeled for political purposes. These celebrations have direct effects upon political mobilization — identifying themselves publicly and proudly as North Africans is subsequently translated into support for political candidates who represent their ethnic group. There exists, in this sense, an overlap between cultural performances and politics. Indeed, the argument can be made that recent Moroccan political mobility is closely related to the unique way in which members of this group have successfully fashioned a series of new Israeli festivals. As we will later see in greater detail, the Moroccans have been exceptionally creative in designing new Israeli cultural events. Of course, the relations between ethnic celebrations and political mobility moves in both directions: for example, political mobilization during election campaigns also brings about a growing sense of ethnic identity, and this in turn results in larger crowds of persons attending events such as the pilgrimage. This dialectic is undoubtedly complex but nonetheless effective: cultural messages have political meanings and vice versa (Weingrod 1985).

There is, finally, an additional political dimension that needs to be considered. This pertains to the interconnections that exist between mystical beliefs in the miraculous powers of saints, on the one hand, and the emergent Israeli ideologies and movements that wed political nationalism with Jewish religious fundamentalism, on the other. The issues here are even more misty and complicated, but their meanings and implications are obviously far-reaching.

The interweaving between ideologies of nationalism and religious fundamentalism began emerging in Israel following the Six Day War in 1967. Briefly summarized, as a result of the Israeli military victory the entire West Bank region of Jordan as well as all of the city of Jerusalem came under Israeli military control. This swift, unexpected military turn of events set off two complementary trends. First, nationalist sentiments urging that Israel retain and annex these territories grew in strength. This viewpoint had long been a central focus of the political platform of a then-minority rightist political party, Herut, who for decades had advanced a more activist policy against the Palestinian Arabs, and who also believed that the West Bank area was a legitimate part of "The Land of Israel." They were joined by other Israelis from the political Left who argued that this new situation presented a historic opportunity to rectify Israel's acute border problems. Although rejecting the doctrine of annexation, the then-dominant Labor party initiated the policy of establishing new Jewish settlements in the West Bank areas.

This political movement was joined—and, in fact, in many ways inspired and led—by a new religious ideology claiming these areas as the historic and "sacred" right of the Jewish people. This was expressed by the zealots of the Gush Emunim movement, who took the settlement of the West Bank to be a holy, divinely inspired act. Although small in number, they undoubtedly constituted a vibrant force (Aronoff 1984; Weissbrod 1982). Moreover, not only were these small religious groups deeply immersed in nationalist political activities, Israel's religious minority was at the same time undergoing a swing toward greater religious orthodoxy (Friedman 1985). This was expressed both symbolically and in daily behavior—to cite several examples, greater emphasis was placed upon observing personal ritual, males and females were segregated in what formerly had been nonorthodox religious schools and youth movements, and there was a turn away from secular studies and greater emphasis placed upon religious training for youngsters. The extreme orthodox minority within the religious population also gained confidence and strength, and this was reinforced by a widely reported interest in religious conversion among some segments of the majority Israeli secular population (Aviad 1983). To be sure, this trend toward what Israelis call "blackening" (the male religious zealots are dressed in black clothing; hence, the term *blackening*) was not unique to Jews in Israel. Fundamentalist religious movements have been increasingly influential among Palestinian Arabs, in the neighboring Middle Eastern Arab countries as well as elsewhere throughout the world. Fundamentalism among Jews undoubtedly derives from many of the same factors that generate this trend among other populations, although it also springs from some of the unique features influencing present-day Israeli society.[9]

These two increasingly powerful currents—political nationalism and religious fundamentalism—subsequently met, and to some extent merged, within the Israeli political system. Following the 1977 national elections, the more nationalist Likud replaced Labor as the major political force, and it has since formed governments together with the religious political parties, including several that are fundamentalist in orientation. This coalition has undoubtedly been an important cultural as well as political force; it may not be the main or preeminent current in Israeli society, and yet there can be little doubt that it has considerable strength and influence. In addition, these right-of-center political parties draw their support from the same broad segments of the Israeli population: as various studies have shown, both the nationalist and the fundamentalist parties have appealed to the Middle Eastern origin, lower socioeconomic portions of the electorate.[10] Indeed, the success of these parties has been in developing popular support among the broad mass of Israeli voters, both secular and religious. What this lower-income, generally less well-educated, and mainly Middle Eastern sector share is a certain basic conservatism, an emphasis upon patriotism and sacred Jewish values, persisting resentment against the previous Ashkenazic elites, as well as militant anti-Arab sentiment.

Against this much-simplified background the *hillula*'s broader political significance can begin to be gauged. The growing popularity of *zaddikim* and their *hilluloth* is connected with the rise of nationalist and fundamentalist sentiments (Cohen 1983). Belief in the miraculous power of saints is widespread among some of the same populations whose outlook has become more nationalist and orthodox. The pilgrims who gather at the cemetery are drawn primarily from the lower-income, North African sections of the population; Rabbi Chouri's *hillula* is, as was emphasized previously, a "popular" outpouring of persons, just as the political movements described here also have "popular" appeal. Seen more broadly, right-wing politicians and black-clothed rabbis now appear together on the same public platforms, often voicing programs or ideologies that complement one another. During election campaigns in particular, these two streams frequently overlap: photographs of politicians embracing saintly persons appear in the media, and some political parties flash scenes of holy shrines on the television screen as part of their electioneering tactics. In the specific case of Rabbi Chouri's *hillula*, it is not by chance that the *zaddik*'s grandson is politically active in a religious orthodox political party that campaigns heavily among North African voters, and receives substantial voting support from them.

This latter remark brings us back to the pilgrimage itself. The argument is not that the participants are all, or even in their majority, supporters of fundamentalist or nationalist political parties; there is no evidence for such a conclusion. Nor is it maintained that taking part in the *hillula* directly or inevitably leads the pilgrims to affiliate with these broad-scaled movements. Again, there are no data to prove this supposition, and it may also be that persons separate their participation in a memorial celebration from their political party affiliation. On the other hand, however, there is a certain congruence between a mystical belief in the power of saints and these political movements: at the least, there are no serious contradictions between, say, patriotic nationalism and believing in the *zaddik*'s ability to cure illness, or greater orthodoxy in religious practices and lighting candles at the *zaddik*'s grave. The same sensibility is there, and as a consequence, these different currents all finally flow in the same direction.

5 Comparison

I

This has been a lengthy journey—from Jerba to Beersheba, rabbi to saint, and from a small family gathering in the cemetery to a giant pilgrimage. The focus throughout has been upon Rabbi Chouri and his *hillula*; nearly all of the emphasis has been upon a single instance, a unique chain of circumstances. There are, surely, many advantages to be gained from the study of a single case. Discovering and then analyzing the "right case" often suggests new insights into a broad range of different yet broadly analogous circumstances; when properly presented the rich coloring of detail may come close to, even touch, the edges of reality; and then it leads to wider, deeper understandings.

At the same time, however, the single case has obvious limitations. One immediately wonders how idiosyncratic it really is, and whether, in truth, it merely represents itself. Cases always differ, and the details of the one, no matter how well illuminated, may have no real relationship to another. What is more, this narrow vision often inhibits seeing wider, more general trends and processes; the fascination with ripe detail is in this sense not necessarily so illuminating. No matter how rich and informative it may appear to be, at some point the single case needs to be viewed in broader comparative perspectives.

Two lines of comparison are pursued in this final chapter. The first examines the process by which additional new saints and shrines are, quite literally, being created; and the second moves to the more general issue of ceremonies of ethnic renewal, and contrasts these pilgrimages with other forms of ethnic celebration both in Israel and other multiethnic societies. Some additional strands are also followed, but these two are the major motifs in this concluding comparative review.

II

A number of recent studies have documented the ways in which new shrines and *zaddikim* have been emerging in a variety of Israeli locales. As in the case of Rabbi Chouri and his *hillula*, these are all exceptional, effervescent cultural explosions; although they appear to be variations on several basic themes, each is extraordinary in itself. What they show, among a great many other things, is that Rabbi Chouri's *hillula* is in no way an isolated case.

Issachar Ben-Ami's research on these topics has been particularly comprehensive and instructive (Ben-Ami 1981; 1984). His general topic is Moroccan Jews and the ways in which they have transferred their traditions of "saint veneration" from Morocco to Israel. He describes two different ways in which new holy places as well as new *zaddikim* have become recognized and subsequently popularized. One process consists of the immigrants "adopting" and thereby reviving an ancient, authoritative shrine—or, as he puts it, "the 'annexation' of Holy Places by the Moroccan Jews" (1981, 302). Ben-Ami describes the scene graphically:

> They flock to the cave of Elijah the Prophet, to the grave of Rabbi Shimon Bar Yochai, to that of Rabbi Meir Ba'al Hanes, and later to the Wailing Wall and to Shimeon the Just. Observations at these sites reveals a massive presence of Moroccan Jews. (1981, 302)

Having become "annexed," these famed sites are thought to have magical, restorative powers; the believers gather there throughout the year to pray, light candles, and plea for God and the *zaddik*'s intervention on their behalf. These have, in other words, become accepted shrines for the Moroccan newcomers. The sites mentioned by Ben-Ami have long been famous as centers of pilgrimage and prayer, and in most cases they also are situated within or close to large population centers such as Jerusalem and Haifa.

In addition, a number of new shrines have also been located or created de novo in outlying Israeli development towns. These are, as was previously pointed out, places where the local population is primarily composed of Moroccan Jews. This process is well-illustrated in the shrine of Rabbi Choni Hameagel, a renowned talmudic sage whose grave was lately "discovered" near to the northern Israeli town of Hatzor Hagalilit. According to Ben-Ami's account, the proximity of the grave to the new town prompted the Moroccan residents adopting the site and the *zaddik* as their own. This close association soon led to "visits by the villagers and the establishment of a central *hillula*. The Day of Independence was chosen as the Hillula day par excellence," and the shrine also attracts "a big crowd from the surroundings" on religious festivals and other holidays (Ben-Ami 1981, 322-23). In this manner Rabbi Choni Hameagel has, in effect, become the *zaddik* of Hatzor.

A more eccentric process is described by Yoram Bilu in his account of the "Gate of Paradise" in Beth She'an, another small Israeli town. According to a talmudic tradition the entrance to the biblical Garden of Eden is to be found somewhere in the vicinity of the present-day Beth She'an. Bilu relates that in 1979 a resident of the town announced that he had "discovered this entrance in his back-yard" (Bilu 1984). This discovery was shrouded in mystical elements; "it was precipitated by a series of visitational dreams in which Elijah the Prophet appeared . . . disclosing to him the secret of the place, and guiding him in and out." Shortly thereafter a series of festivites were organized there:

> At the beginning of the month of Ellul the *hillula* for Elijah is celebrated in this place, near the fenced concrete floor which marks the location of the sacred spot. The site has not acquired as yet full legitimization as a pilgrimage center and is hardly known outside Beth She'an. Most of the pilgrims are local inhabitants, mainly from the close neighborhood. (Bilu 1984)

This "Gate of Paradise" is still in an early stage of development; over time one supposes that its magical powers and fame are likely to increase.

The annexation of ancient holy places and uncovering new ones represents one of the ways in which new Israeli shrines and *hilluloth* are being formed. Both Ben-Ami and Bilu have also documented a second process: in a number of striking instances a renowned Moroccan *zaddik* has been magically transported to Israel where new shrines and pilgrimages have developed. These circumstances are, to say the least, remarkable, and they attest once again to the continuing importance of *zaddikim* and celebration in the lives of Moroccan Jews.

The *zaddik* in question is Rabbi David u'Moshe, who, according to Ben-Ami, was among the best known and popular of the Moroccan Jewish saints. The details of his life are unclear; many of the stories that Ben-Ami collected about him assign a Palestinian origin to this charismatic rabbi, but little is known about his actual life (Ben-Ami 1981, 258-88). Nonetheless, his grave in the Moroccan High Atlas region, near the village of Agouim, was a major shrine for Moroccan Jews; the yearly *hillula* at his grave "drew thousands of people from all over Morocco," many of whom camped out at the grave site for lengthy periods of time (Bilu 1984).

> People from all over Morocco flock to the celebration a week before it begins. They remain in the place for a week to a month in an atmosphere of constant exaltation. . . . One of the more significant rituals is the slaughter of sacrificial animals near the grave. When thousands of candles were lit and joined into one great flame, miracles happened. (Ben-Ami 1981, 292)

With this vibrant background and force, it is perhaps not surprising that from among the many Moroccan *zaddikim* it was Rabbi David u'Moshe who was magically transported to Israel! If "miracles happened" in Agouim, then how appropriate that they should continue in Israel.

Two new Israeli shrines dedicated to Rabbi David u'Moshe have been established. The first of these is located in the southern Israeli town of Ashkelon. In the early 1960s a Moroccan immigrant named Shimeon Waknin began organizing a *hillula* to take place on the same day that the pilgrimage to Rabbi David u'Moshe's grave was traditionally held in Morocco. This celebration and the attendant festivities are held in and around a small neighborhood synagogue that bears the rabbi's name, the Synagogue in Memory of Rabbi David u'Moshe. Like the yearly *hillula* in the High Atlas Mountains, this is a lively, in certain respects stunning, celebration; here, too, "it attracts a large crowd, which comes from all over the country" (Ben-Ami 1981, 304). The events of the *hillula* in Ashkelon are modeled after the celebration in Morocco. For example, animal sacrifice has a central role in the Israeli performance. A special sacrificial bull is slaughtered within the synagoguge itself on the day prior to the *hillula*. This is a particularly dramatic moment: "After the slaughterer has examined and checked the innards of the ox," Ben-Ami writes, "he lifts his head and his right arm. This is the long-awaited signal that the ox is Kosher (ritually pure). The audience again bursts out in cries of joy and the women cry *zagharit*" (Ben-Ami 1981, 306). The main celebration honoring the *zaddik* takes place on the following day. The communal meal (during

which parts of the ox as well as other sacrificial animals are consumed)
is the climax of the celebration:

> All through the day things are in motion. People come and look
> around. The old man [Waknin] and his wife transmit their orders
> in loud voices. Immediately following the prayers, more tables and
> chairs are brought in. . . . Soon all the seats are occupied in the
> synagogue, the courtyard, and the club. Many people stand in all
> the passages, and in the street. The women burst out in a mighty
> and continuous singing; one can see groups of women dancing.
> Here and there one also finds groups of musicians, who gather
> a large audience. All this occurs amid laughter and jubilation.
> (Ben-Ami 1981, 306-307)

Ben-Ami goes on to detail a lengthy list of miracles that this zaddik
is said to have performed. Not only is his hillula celebrated in a synagogue in Israel, Rabbi David u'Moshe is now believed to heal the sick
in Ashkelon and Jerusalem, just as he, like other zaddikim, is thought
to protect Israeli soldiers in battle.

The second shrine is even more complex and interesting. This
new holy place is situated in Safad, the old kabalistic center in the
north of Israel, and it is also dedicated to Rabbi David u'Moshe. Its
genesis is inextricably tied with a founder, Avraham Ben Hayim, an
immigrant from Morocco, and a series of dreams. In the early 1970s,
Ben Hayim, who was then employed as a forestry worker, announced
that the zaddik had appeared to him in dreams and instructed him to
build a shrine within his home. These dreams continued, and Ben
Hayim wrote them out in dramatic form, distributing them to Moroccan
synagogues throughout the country. The instructions he received during these dreams were explicit. In his published "Announcements to
the Public," Ben Hayim describes a scene in which the zaddik appeared
to him and spoke:

> I am the man who revealed himself to those who loved me in
> Morocco. I am Rabbi David u'Moshe!!! . . . Why have you deserted
> me, those who left Morocco? Now here I am in the Holy Land,
> and my request is that they renew the Hillula. . . . And now hear
> my words: I left Morocco and came here, because this place is
> Holy and I chose you to be my servant in this Holy work. (Ben-
> Ami 1981, 325)

The repeated publication of dreams and orders from the zaddik generated great interest; in fact, Ben-Ami writes that "this publishing activity

has won his reputation and authority" (ibid., 325). Ben Hayim left his previous employment and has since devoted himself entirely to the *zaddik*. He rebuilt several rooms in and around his home as places of prayer and devotion. Almost immediately pilgrims began to flock to this new holy site: "Within a few years the new place was transformed into a major pilgrimage center," writes Bilu. "All year long it draws a constant flow of supplicants in small numbers, but at the time of the *hillula* a crowd of up to 15,000 pilgrims gathers in the open before the *zaddik*'s room" (Bilu 1984). Ben-Ami's description of this scene is worth repeating:

> The many people who come to the *Hillula* in Safed, organize themselves into small groups, in a courtyard near the house. In one corner there is a roofless room in which candles may be burnt and the people camp out all night long, as was the custom in Morocco. Another innovation is the special room which is devoted only to the saint. In addition many people come to stay one or more nights, for the purpose of healing. (1981, 324)

Like Rabbi Choni Hameagel in Hatzor and Rabbi Chayim Chouri in Beersheba, Rabbi David u'Moshe, perhaps the most powerful of the Moroccan-Jewish saints, has become an authentic Israeli *zaddik*.[1]

The final example differs from the others, although in many respects it is similar to Rabbi Chouri. This is the case of the most recent (and also most famous) of the new Israeli *zaddikim*, Rabbi Israel Abouhatzeira, or as he is popularly known, the Baba Sali. Like Rabbi Chouri he was a real, contemporary person who has become a saint. Rabbi Abouhatzeira was a scion of the most distinguished Moroccan-Jewish rabbinic family; his grandfather, Rabbi Yaacov Abouhatzeira, was a well-known talmudist whose grave near Alexandria, Egypt, has for decades been an important pilgrimage site for Moroccan Jews, and various other members of his family have attained scholarly as well as political fame and high status.

The details of his long life, even in bare outline form, immediately indicate his great personal powers. As a young man in Morocco Rabbi Abouhatzeira gained a reputation as a scholar, and equally important, as a miracle worker and healer. In 1964 he immigrated to Israel; he was then already in his seventies, but continued to lead an energetic and productive life. A number of years following his arrival he and his family settled in the small Israeli town of Netivoth, not far from Beersheba, where he organized and headed a *yeshiva*. His home in Netivoth soon became an active pilgrimage center; persons flocked there to receive his blessing and counsel on a variety of topics ranging from illness to financial transactions. Interestingly, his followers included not only Moroccans but also many orthodox Ashkenazi Jews among whom his miraculous powers were also recognized. (The Baba Sali was famous for blessing bottles of water or other liquids that then were believed to possess healing power.) By the time of his death in 1984 at the age of ninety-four, Rabbi Abouhatzeira's fame had spread widely and his followers undoubtedly numbered in the many thousands. The Baba Sali had become a *zaddik* during his own lifetime, and it was therefore not surprising that immediately following his death his grave site became a holy place. He was buried in a large tomb situated outside of Netivoth, and the yearly *hillula* to his grave, organized by his controversial son and heir, Baruch, has already become a national-level pilgrimage site and holy shrine.[2]

This brief catalogue hardly does justice to the events themselves: each of the instances described, from the "Gate of Paradise" to Baba Sali, is a small world unto itself. What is certainly made clear, however, is that the *hillula* in Beersheba is only one in a series of comparable cases: neither the pilgrimage to Rabbi Chouri's grave nor the way in which it developed is entirely unique. To be sure, the identity of each new *zaddik* varies widely — some, such as Rabbi Chouri and the Baba Sali, were renowned historical personages, others like Choni Hameagel were ancient charismatic figures who have been revived, and still others like Rabbi David u'Moshe have been mysteriously transferred from Morocco to Israel. The key point is that in each of these cases an authentic saint has been found or adopted, and the new *kadosh* then becomes the central figure in a new holy shrine and pilgrimage. A Holy Land indeed!

There surely are powerful, pulsating forces that energize this continuing process by which new saints are being created. The sources of this vitality are diverse and complex: they are rooted, at the least, in a mystical religious orientation, a culturally defined view of health and healing, nostalgia for older ceremonial traditions, the immigrant experience of breaking with the past and re-creating the present, as well as a strong sense of ethnic group identification. The comparative analysis of these events is still to be undertaken. The problems inherent in such a comparison are many and complex; the data are far from complete, and these still-unfolding dramas also take new and unpredicted directions.[3] Nevertheless, even a cursory review of the cases mentioned begins to suggest some tantalizing hints: there seems to be a distinctive pattern to the way these new saints and pilgrimages have emerged.

At least four of the elements in this pattern can be listed. First, in each of the cases a particular individual or a small group of persons plays the role of "entrepreneur" in initiating and then continuing to develop the celebration of a new saintly figure. Examples come quickly to mind: Rabbi Chouri's sons, Shimeon Waknin in Ashkelon, and Avraham ben Hayim in Safed, or Baruch Abouhatzeira, the Baba Sali's son. They appear as devout, modest, and yet inspired men who are motivated by deep personal and religious impulses; moreover, with the exception of Baruch Abouhatzeira none of them claims to possess saintly power or is recognized by others to be a charismatic figure. Second, it is obvious from these descriptions that North African Jewish immigrants, and Moroccans in particular, are overwhelmingly involved in these events. The prevalence of members of this group is not at all surprising in the light of the great historic power of saints and pilgrimages in Morocco; this is a point that was previously emphasized, and there is no need to repeat it again. On the other hand, traditions of *zaddikim* and pilgrimages to their graves are also a part of the heritage of other Middle Eastern Jewish groups—notably Jews from Syria, Iraq, and Kurdistan—and there is no evidence that they have renewed these activities in Israel. Why this should be poses intriguing problems that merit future study. Third, these new holy places and *hilluloth* have all developed in small, peripheral Israeli cities and towns. Beersheba, Ashkelon, Hatzor Hagalilit, and Netivoth are far from the major Israeli population centers. This may be explained by the fact that Moroccans in particular are packed densely into these outlying peripheral zones and also by the greater power that ethnic identification may have in these small towns (Spilerman and Habib 1976). Ethnic boundaries are likely to be stronger, and ethnic traditions longer lasting, in small towns such as Safad or Ashkelon when compared to large urban centers like Tel Aviv or Jerusalem. Furthermore, as Ben-Ari and Bilu suggest, these new *zaddikim* provide a way in which the mainly North African residents become more closely attached to their communities (1987). Finally, the trend appears to be one in which a particular *zaddik* becomes associated with a particular place. Rabbi Chouri is the "saint of Beersheba" just as Rabbi Choni Hameagel has become the "saint of Hatzor." This does not mean that pilgrims from other places do not attend these sites, but rather that the local population has a special relationship with the *zaddik* of their own town and his *hillula*. This is reminiscent of the traditional Moroccan pattern, in which nearly every Jewish community had its own saint and *hillula*. Israel's "saint map," to borrow Bilu's term, has been rapidly expanding, and it is likely to continue to do so in the future.

III

In addition to this process of creating new shrines and saints, there is a second major pole of contrast and comparison: all of the *hilluloth* described draw together large crowds of North African, and more particularly Moroccan, immigrants, and they therefore can properly be thought of as ceremonies of ethnic renewal. This term was defined in the previous chapter: it highlights a class of events, or better, public occasions, during which members of a particular country or place-of-origin group join together to perform joint activities that celebrate their past and present. The problem that remains is to consider the distinctly ethnic features of these celebrations within this wider comparative perspective.

One useful way to proceed is to compare these pilgrimages with other celebrations that have only lately come to the fore in Israel. During the past two decades a number of additional, specifically ethnic demonstrations have been organized; these are day-long festivities that often include tens of thousands of persons who join together under a particular ethnic banner. They include, for example, large public festivals organized by Jews from Kurdistan, Persia, Ethiopia, Yemen, and not the least, Morocco. The original, and in certain respects, most successful of these events is a Moroccan celebration called the *mimouna*. The process by which what in Morocco had been a merry family fete was successfully transformed into a national Moroccan-Israeli holiday — a ceremony of ethnic renewal par excellence — deserves careful retelling.

In its traditional Moroccan context *mimouna* was a light-hearted, happy springtime celebration (an expression of "gaiety, spontaneity and a sense of well-being," is the way Goldberg describes it) (1978, 77). It was a relatively new holiday — Ben Ami's research indicates that there was no record of it before the eighteenth century — and the derivation of the term itself is not clear. Various Jewish authorities have linked *mimouna* with the rhyming Hebrew term *emunah*, meaning belief or faith, while others have seen a connection with the name of the famous Jewish sage Maimonides who sojourned in Morocco during the Middle Ages (Goldberg 1978, 81). Whatever its origins, the celebration commonly took place on the day following Passover — or to be more precise, *mimouna* began on the evening of the final day of the week-long Passover celebration and continued through the following day. Although the details vary from one Jewish community to the next, the same themes seem to run through the festivities. In the evening young girls and boys dressed in festive clothes promenaded through the streets; in some places Jews appeared as Muslims, and in general the fete contained elements of masquerade ("The little girls and lasses dress in an 'ajama. . . . The young men wear Muslim clothing and tour about the streets with mandolins") (Goldberg 1978, 76). Families visited with one another and exchanged blessings with close friends; special festive foods were prepared, and quantities of mahia, a kind of arak, also were consumed. The following day was typically an occasion for family gatherings that took place in the countryside; Goldberg writes that "the day of *mimouna* is usually spent outside the city picnicking in a wood or garden, or near a source of water" (1978, 77). The atmosphere was cheerful and relaxed: this was a time when prospective young suitors met and peeked at one another, and marriage matches were often made during the *mimouna* festivities.

There is no indication that, following their immigration, these holiday traditions were observed in the new, secular and in most respects culturally hostile Israeli atmosphere; like other newcomers, Moroccan Jews were instructed to dispose of their former traditions and "become Israelis." Until the late 1960s only a handful of Moroccans living in Israel celebrated *mimouna* in a style similar to the traditional celebrations in Fez or Meknes, or for that matter, in any form at all. However, in the late 1960s *mimouna* began its Israeli revival. The process was not spontaneous but instead the result of deliberate planning and organization. A tiny group of politically active Moroccan immigrants apparently conceived the idea of sponsoring a large *mimouna* celebration; they formed a committee, received the support and encouragement of a number of important individuals and groups, and announced that the first Israeliwide *mimouna* celebration would be held on the day following the end of Passover. The main festivity was planned for Jerusalem, with smaller gatherings to be held near various Moroccan population concentrations in the north and south of the country. North Africans were invited to come and take part in a large picnic and celebration—to eat traditional foods, sing, and dance in a festive manner—and various Israeli dignitaries, such as the prime minister and chief rabbis, were also sent invitations. To the organizer's surprise, large and enthusiastic crowds flocked to these celebrations; the areas laid out for picnickers were soon covered with family groups who appeared to be relishing the occasion. Indeed, for the first time Moroccan immigrants who previously may have sought to identify themselves as "from the South of France" were joining together under a specifically Moroccan ethnic banner. If anything, they had come in order to join in a public demonstration of their "Moroccanness". These first celebrations were a success, and they set the pattern for the now-yearly festivities that have, in effect, become an Israeli national holiday.

During the 1980s the *mimouna* celebration characteristically begins with a revival of the traditional evening gatherings: in Moroccan neighborhoods throughout Israel festive meals are prepared and families and friends visit one another. Some of these visits are well-publicized "media events"—various political notables take the occasion to circulate among the Moroccan crowds, and the television cameras record the Israeli president or prime minister sitting around a sumptuous table together with the Moroccan hosts. On the following day the scene shifts to the Sachar gardens, a large park in Jerusalem located near to the Knesseth, Israel's parliament. Crowds of picnickers and revelers begin to arrive in the late morning. A large stage, replete with flags, decorations, and booming loudspeakers, is set up in the center of the park, and not far away a number of huge tents also are erected. These tents are used to house exhibitions of ethnic folk arts; the largest is reserved for the Moroccans, but there are also tents that record the art and music of Jews from Kurdistan, Georgia, South America, and Ethiopia. The crowds—as many as fifty thousand persons are likely to attend—circulate around these tents, and between grilling meat they pause to sing traditional tunes, dance, play games of chance, or just loll in the sun. The formal program of activities begins early in the afternoon. Groups of performers sing and dance on the central stage, and no less important, leading Israeli political figures address the crowd. The president, prime minister, chief-of-staff of the Army, and the chief rabbis all make an appearance, and the leaders of Israel's numerous political parties also walk among the North African participants. *Mimouna*'s overt political tones have in recent years been strongly felt:

during the celebrations in 1981 the then-prime minister, Menachem Begin, was cheered enthusiastically, while the leader of the opposition Labor party was booed and even jostled by the crowd. Later, when the stage appearances have ended, the crowd begins to leave, with some families remaining to play and picnic until late in the day.

A suggestive article by Harvey Goldberg shows how, in Morocco, mimouna provided a format for a symbolic reversal of status: Jews dressed as Muslims; and they, the weak, momentarily appeared to be powerful (1978). Mimouna as reinterpreted in Israel also expresses a process of change in status: Moroccans, who in Israel had been relegated to low-ranked positions and were the butt of prejudice, have now become hosts to the Israeli national elite. As symbolized by the tents, the Moroccans also wish to be the patrons of other ethnic groups, all of whom now publicly demonstrate their ethnic identities. Mimouna has, in effect, been an important force in Israel's cultural transformation: the move from social assimilation to cultural pluralism is particularly well expressed in this resurgent festival (Weingrod 1979).

It should come as no surprise to learn that mimouna has become the prototypical Israeli ethnic celebration. A number of other immigrant groups have lately developed their own ethnic holidays, and they have consciously been modeled after the success of mimouna. For example, Jews from Kurdistan now sponsor a traditional festival known as the seherrana. Like the Moroccan mimouna, the Kurdish seherrana had been a springtime picnic traditionally held on the last day of Passover; however, since in Israel the Moroccans had already preempted that day (and the attendant publicity) the Kurdish organizing committee moved the seherrana to the holiday of Succoth that takes place in the fall! Thus for the past decade or so Kurdish Jews have been gathering together in large numbers to celebrate their own holiday (Halper and Abromovitz 1984). A rural site is chosen—near a Kurdish village or a small town with a concentration of Kurdish Jews—and thousands of persons join together in eating, singing traditional melodies, and listening to speeches delivered by Israeli politicians. To cite another example, Persian immigrants have also recently gathered together to celebrate their day, called Ruz-e-begh. (Judith Goldstein, who has studied the emergence of ethnic symbols among Persian Jews, wryly calls this "the Persian mimouna.") This festival is held on the day following Passover, when upwards of twenty thousand Persian Jews gather in a park in the city of Ramath Gan. Finally, the most recent group of immigrants to Israel, the Ethiopian Jews, have also organized their own renewal ceremony: a traditional Ethiopian holy day, the *Sigd*, is now observed in Israel by communal prayers and fasting. Ethiopians from all over Israel gather together on a hill overlooking Jerusalem, where, following a morning of prayers and addresses by religious leaders, they descend in silent procession to the holy Western Wall. Various Israeli dignitaries also attend the *Sigd* ceremony, and like the others this event is also widely reported in the Israeli media (Ben-Dor 1987).

Comparing ethnic festivals such as the *mimouna* or *seherrana* with memorial celebrations like Rabbi Chouri's or the Baba Sali's *hillula* reveals a number of interesting contrasts. Both of these forms of celebration share certain features. They all are occasions during which ethnic group identification and solidarity are strongly enhanced; the revival of "old country" traditions of food and song, language and belief, has the effect of renewing ties to the participants' ethnic past and present. Of course, celebrations like *mimouna* are much more explicit, robust ethnic events in comparison with, say, the *hillula* of Rabbi David u'Moshe; the latter has a more implicit ethnic message, while the former is practically designed as a vehicle for mobilizing collective feelings.

These contrasts are worth pursuing. The political features of *mimouna* or the *Sigd* celebration are also much more clear and explicit than the *hilluloth*. As was emphasized, these new ethnic festivals were not only inspired and organized by small groups of politically active persons, they were immediately perceived to be successful frameworks for political organization. Israeli political leaders from all of the parties in the political spectrum attend festivals such as the *seherrana* and *Ruz-e-begh*; in fact these renewal ceremonies have played vital roles in these ethnic groups' recent upward political mobility. On the other hand, overt political and political-party expressions are generally absent from the memorial celebrations where large crowds flock to the *zaddik's* grave. As was pointed out in the description of Rabbi Chouri's *hillula*, the mayor of Beersheba and other local politicians rarely make an appearance at the cemetery, and the only political figures who do attend are several Tunisians who live in the area. This is also the case (with one notable exception) with the other *hilluloth* that were described previously. How can these differences be explained?

The contrast between these two kinds of celebrations — *mimouna* or *seherrana*, on the one hand, and *hilluloth*, on the other — is that the first can be more easily transmuted into a political gathering, while the latter are inherently more difficult to recast. *Mimouna* is an almost ideal cultural vessel for new social and political purposes; both its form and contents are fluid and light-hearted, and it is not closely bound up with a firm set of beliefs and explicit ritual practices. It is plastic and pliable, and as a consequence *mimouna* and festivals like it have been successfully reinterpreted in the new Israeli environment. The crowds that gather to picnic in the parks are honored and pleased, rather than offended, when political leaders arrive to, in effect, campaign for their support. The *hilluloth*, on the other hand, have a tighter religious and symbolic structure, and their traditional meanings are not so easily bent and reshaped. As we have seen, the Beersheba cemetery is perceived as an inappropriate place to conduct a political rally. There is something offensive, out of joint, in attempting to merge religious exaltation with narrow political appeals.

There is, however, an exception to this rule: it is, in fact, a resounding exception. The Baba Sali's son and heir, Baruch Abouhatzeira (or, as he is now known, Baba Baruch) has succeeded in directly mixing political and mystical-religious motifs. The Baba Sali's yearly *hillula* has quickly become both a memorial celebration *and* a political rally. This is readily apparent in the way that this pilgrimage has been designed. In the space close to the Baba Sali's shrine — a large, Moorish-styled structure that covers the *zaddik*'s grave — a new permanent stage was built, and during the afternoon of the *hillula* a selection of Israel's national political and religious leaders gather there to address the throngs of believers. Even though the speeches do not have direct political-party labels, this is an obvious political demonstration: as might be expected, all of the speakers and other guests are drawn from the right-of-center Israeli political spectrum. The crowds that gather to listen to the prime minister or the chief rabbis seem to maintain an interest in the presentations, and later they return to lighting candles or eating their festive meal. In this instance , direct political elements have been bound together with a mystical religious performance. As with each of the events presented, it will be interesting to see how this particular design develops in the coming years.

IV

This brings us to the final frame of comparison. Thus far the emphasis has exclusively been upon Israeli celebrations and their many dimensions. Once again, there are both advantages and disadvantages to focusing upon a single society. Comparing festivities within one society to some extent limits and thereby controls the number of factors that must be taken into account when making comparisons, although, on the other hand, emphasizing a single society has the distinct disadvantage of ruling out relevant events that are taking place in other sociocultural systems. This latter consideration is important: it is valuable to contrast Israeli ethnic renewal ceremonies with comparable festivities that take place in other multiethnic societies.

There is, in fact, a rich literature that describes and analyzes events of this kind. To cite only a few examples, already in the 1950s Lloyd Warner presented a fascinating analysis of a Fourth of July celebration in an American town in New England. Among other things, Warner's analysis shows how various minority groups were represented, or sought to present themselves, in a grand, citywide pageant that wended its way through the streets of Yankee City (1959). In a more contemporary American vein, Wiggins's depiction of the "Juneteenth" celebrations is a marvelous rendering of how American blacks reinterpreted the same occasion—Independence Day—in keeping with their own history, experience and traditions (Wiggins 1982). To move to some different locales, Frank Manning's depiction of Caribbean festivals (Carnival in Antigua and the Cricket Cup Match in Bermuda) presents vivid depictions of how these complex cultural events are inextricably tied to the structures of local society and politics (1983). Similarly, Roberto Da Matta's fine analysis of Carnival in Rio de Janiero, and Eva Hunt's study of Indian-mestizo relationships as these are encapsulated in local political assemblies, also uncover vibrant events where, among other themes, ethnic-group ties become solidified (Manning 1983). All of these studies—and a great many others—explore the relations between culture and politics in modern multiethnic societies. However, if a single recent work along these lines stands out for its richness and complexity, it surely is Abner Cohen's studies of a Carnival in London. His analysis of these events has many similarities to the themes pursued in this book, and it therefore affords particular comparative possibilities.

Cohen's analysis of what became famous as London's Notting Hill Carnival is a well-told study in the interrelations between microsociology, politics, and culture. In a series of articles he traces the complicated process by which, in a period of little more than a decade, a tiny local initiative to organize an English-style street fair ("the Notting Hill Annual Fayre") was literally swept away into an enormous celebration led by West Indians and attended by hundreds of thousands of persons, an event that not only had a surging life of its own but also galvanized street drama and political struggle into one extraordinary mix. To put it in his own words, the study is about the "process by which a group engaged in political confrontation mobilized its culture and its communal relationships to coordinate its corporate action in the struggle for power" (1980, 67). It is a fascinating tale.

The analysis ranges over a relatively brief but turbulent period of time, from 1965 through 1979. Cohen divides this particular "seamless web" into three different periods or stages. During the first stage (1965-1970) a local Notting Hill resident, Rhaunee Laslett, was inspired by the idea of having a local carnival that would bring together all of the great mixture of persons who were living in this old, rather decrepit working class zone of London (the carnival would, she thought, "bring some colour, warmth and happiness to a grim and depressed neighborhood") (1982, 25). The carnival was first staged on a long weekend in August. It included representation from a cross section of Notting Hill:

> There were dancers from the Ukraine, Cyprus and India, and a variety of musical groups including a small West Indian Band that had been formed in a pub. . . . The procession was led by an Englishman who rode on a stagecoach masquerading as Queen Victoria. (1980, 67)

This first carnival was a success, and in the years that followed it was held again on the same date. Although the specifically West Indian component of the carnival was growing, what characterized this initial period was working-class cooperation across ethnic lines. The cultural formats of carnival were English: "Most of the forms of music, drama, poetry, dancing and masquerading employed in the carnival at that period were cultural forms shared between West Indians and Britons" (1982, 29); indeed, "the interaction and cooperating during the months of preparation for the carnival" seemed to be effectively "bringing about communion across the colour lines" (1982, 29).

In its next phase, from 1970 until 1975, the carnival not only grew enormously but also became almost exclusively West Indian. Cohen explains the West Indian dominance as the result of several factors. First, many of the white residents were moving to other zones of London; the West Indians, who were primarily poor renters of rooms and flats, had few other alternatives and they therefore remained and became the largest local group. Second, violence beween West Indian youngsters and the police flared into rioting, and this also polarized the formerly united working-class residents ("The confrontation frightened Mrs. Laslett and led her to cancel the carnival. . . . But the carnival movement had a momentum of its own; other local leaders took over") (1982, 33). Third, some of the local West Indian artists and political activists deliberately recast the street celebration from an "English Fayre" to a Trinidadian carnival: carnival was, after all, a living part of *their* tradition, and increasingly they staged the London event as a West Indian, specifically Trinidadian celebration:

> West Indian Londoners adopted the Trinidad artistic conventions but used them to dramatise different messages. . . . In London towards the end of the 1960's and certainly in the 1970's . . . it served as a medium for expressing and organizing protest, resistance and counteraction, first on the part of a working-class section, consisting of both white and black groups, later on the part of West Indians only. (1982, 34)

The carnival then became, as in Trinidad, a matter of parade, procession, and above all, steel bands throbbing through the streets, playing in massed rhythms. Cohen shows how the organization of steel bands directed the energies of a great many neighborhood youngsters; "like a football team, every band has its supporters who follow its performance during the year and who jump behind it on carnival day. They support it financially, physically and morally" (1980, 72).

In its third phase, 1976-1979, the carnival's cultural idiom again began to shift. By then ten years old, it had become a major London "event": the Notting Hill Carnival was picked up and publicized by the media, and the attendance soared to include an estimated quarter-million persons (1980, 74). Larger numbers of West Indian youngsters began to take part; they represented, according to Cohen, "a new generation of West Indian teenagers, born and educated in Britain. It is a generation of alienated, disillusioned, demoralized and rebellious youth, whose plight has affected their parents, souring their relation to British society" (1980, 74). These youngsters not only fought with the police, they also introduced new styles and cultural elements of their own into the carnival; more specifically, the carnival's music shifted to the beat of Reggae tunes, and it also expressed the moods and religious orientation of Rastafarianism, the Caribbean religion that had been transferred to England:

> Reggae and Rastafarianism gave British-born West Indian youth a world view, political philosophy, an exclusive language, rituals in the form of special appearance and lifestyle, ecstasy through music, dancing and marijuana smoking. More significantly, together they have become articulating principals for the formation of primary neighborhood groups, who move in the slums of the inner city to attend one sound system or another. (1980, 75)

Cohen concludes by noting that the carnival, with its "immense political and cultural potentialities, has proved efficacious in many respects. It has infused collective consciousness among West Indians and has continuously drawn public attention to the plight of West Indian youth." It is, moreover, a social occasion "for reunion among friends and acquaintances who would otherwise not meet. . . . These political-organizational functions of the carnival are in a dialectical relation with the cultural, artistic forms of the carnival" (1980, 79).

Contrasting the carnival in London with the *mimouna* and *hilluloth* in Israel is more than just an exercise in comparison; the similarities are striking, and they suggest a number of interesting conclusions. Many of the circumstances follow similar themes: the West Indians who directed the carnival and turned it into a national event are immigrants or the second-generation descendants of immigrants, just as the Moroccans who reinterpreted *mimouna* also are immigrants. There is obviously something about the status of immigrant that makes ceremonies of this kind important and meaningful. Both the West Indians and the Moroccans are (or were) low-status groups who, at least to some degree, deliberatley utilized some of their own native cultural formats as vehicles for enhancing group solidarity and advancing up the socioeconomic mobility ladder. These festivities are not only resurrections of folk arts or expressions of folklore, they also have important social, economic, and especially political meanings. Some of the similarities in the process of cultural selection are especially interesting: like *mimouna*, the carnival is a uniquely open, elastic cultural format that can be stretched and moved in various novel directions as it is introduced into a new social environment. Bringing steel bands to central London was as inspired an idea as making *mimouna*, with its relaxed picnic and Moroccan delicacies, into an Israeli national holiday.

Both of these events exemplify the power of ceremonies of ethnic renewal to not only revive customs and enhance social solidarity, but also to project immigrants and other minorities onto the national center stage. This is a fascinating process that continues to take place in many societies, and there is much to be learned from studying these rapidly changing occasions.

Finally, these comparisons also provide an indication of the continuing power of celebration and festivity in modern urban societies. This theme is particularly well developed in Victor Turner's work (Turner 1982), and it finds corroboration here. It has often been maintained that modern urban societies are places where genuine festivities are being replaced by staged "media events," or where persons attend to the media rather than directly taking part in public performances and rituals. The vibrant celebrations that have been described in this book indicate a different path: these festivities and others like them are authentic, powerful, and filled with personal and group emotion. The *hillula* in Beersheba belongs to this class of contemporary celebration. Rabbi Chayim Chouri has become the saint of Beersheba, and in the process his mystic powers have produced a brilliant, wide-ranging festival.

Notes

Chapter 2. Text

1. According to Jewish tradition a day is measured from sundown to sunset. The celebrations at the cemetery usually begin on the morning of *kaf-daled*, the day before the anniversary of Rabbi Chouri's death, and reach their climax that evening, the actual day on which he died. In addition to the day of the *hillula* itself, some persons visit the *zaddik's* grave throughout the year. These visits usually take place in the early morning hours, frequently on a Tuesday or Thursday, which are the days when portions of the Bible are read in the synagogue during the morning prayers. The pilgrims come singly or in small family groups, and they commonly go there to pray for good health or good fortune in a new undertaking.

2. How much money is actually collected at a *hillula*, and how the money is then used, is a topic of endless speculation and gossip. There often are exaggerated ideas regarding the amounts that enter the collection box, and there also are whispered allegations about who benefits from these sums. In the early years of Rabbi Chouri's *hillula*, money placed in the small wooden box that stands on the grave was used to maintain and beautify the shrine; a committee of notables, including the rabbi's sons, decided how these funds would be used. More recently some of the funds are also allocated to the Beersheba *yeshiva* named after Rabbi Chouri, which has become the main center of activities celebrating the *zaddik* and his mystical power.

3. Two books devoted to Rabbi Chouri have been published in Hebrew. The first, written by Matzliach and Chadad, is a compilation including biographical facts and miracle tales. The second book was written by Shushan Chouri, one of the rabbi's grandsons, and it includes a more extensive recounting of miracle tales, as well as numerous photographs and other documentary material.

Chapter 3. Performance

1. Recent studies of saints and pilgrimages include the following:
   M. J. Sallnow, *Pilgrims of the Atlas*, (Washington, D.C.: Smithsonian
   Institution Press) 1987; W. A. Christian, *Apparitions in Late Medieval
   and Renaissance Spain*, (Princeton: Princeton University Press) 1981;
   B. Myerhoff, *Peyote Hunt: The Sacred Journey of the Huichol Indians*,
   (Ithaca: Cornell University Press) 1974; E. Allen Morinis, *Pilgrimages in the Hindu Tradition*, (Delhi: Oxford University Press)
   1984; D. Eickelman, *Moroccan Islam*, (Austin: University of Texas
   Press), 1976.
2. This custom has recently been changed. Rather than conducting the
   seuda at the *zaddik's* home, the evening festivities are now carried
   on at the *yeshiva* named after Rabbi Chouri. This event is publicized
   and everyone is invited to attend—in principle, it is no longer a
   closed "Tunisian affair." In fact, however, it is mainly the Tunisians
   who continue to take part.
3. This term—"contested cultural performance"—is used by Abner
   Cohen in his analysis of how the design of the Notting Hill Carnival
   evolved through negotiation. See A. Cohen, 1982.

Chapter 4. Process

1. This literature is written in French, Hebrew, and English, and it
   includes several fine monographs by both historians and social
   anthropologists. Among others, research in North Africa by Abitbol,
   Ben-Ami, Deshen, Goldberg, Rosen, Stillman, and Udovitch and
   Valensi can be cited; published studies on North Africans in Israel
   includes work by Bar Yosef, Bensimon, Bilu, Deshen, Goldberg,
   Shokeid, Weingrod, and Willner.
2. The "bittersweet" experiences of North African immigrants in Israel
   during the 1950s are well documented in a series of studies. See for
   example, H. Goldberg, *From Cave Dwellers to Citrus Growers*, (Cambridge: Cambridge University Press) 1972; M. Shokeid, *The Dual
   Heritage*, (Manchester: Manchester University Press) 1971; A. Weingrod, *Reluctant Pioneers*, (Ithaca: Cornell University Press) 1966; and
   D. Willner, *Nation Building and Community in Israel*, (Princeton:
   Princeton University Press), 1965.

3. These data appear in J. Shuval, 1956. Problems of prejudice and discrimination in Israel are discussed in S. Smooha, *Israel: Pluralism and Conflict*, (Berkeley: University of California Press), 1978.

4. A great deal of research has been done on the topic of social mobility with particular emphasis upon Middle Eastern groups. Two recent studies can be cited: Judah Matras's "Intergenerational Social Mobility and Ethnic Organization in the Jewish Population of Israel" and Eliezer Ben-Raphael's "Social Mobility and Ethnic Awareness," both in A. Weingrod, ed., *Studies in Israeli Ethnicity: After the Ingathering*, (New York: Gordon and Breach), 1985.

5. See Y. Peres (1985) for a brief review of recent patterns of interethnic marriage.

6. There is an enormous anthropologiccl literature that places emphasis upon the persistence of beliefs, values, world-views, and ethos over long time periods. In curious ways this has lately been given a new impetus through the ideas and influence of Levi-Strauss and the interest in "symbolic anthropology."

7. The manner in which large public ceremonies become the focus for social, political, and religious themes is given powerful expression in Max Gluckman's analyses of African "rituals of rebellion" (see Gluckman 1963). In a recent article Abeles makes use of this perspective in an analysis of contemporary French political ritual (Abeles 1988).

8. The importance of ethnicity in Israeli national elections is analyzed in a number of articles included in A. Arian, *The Elections in Israeli 1981*, (Tel Aviv: Ramot Publishing) 1983. See in particular articles by Shamir and Arian, and Herzog.

9. These themes are particularly well developed in studies of contemporary Iran. See, for example, M. J. Fisher, *Iran: From Religious Dispute to Revolution*, (Cambridge: Harvard University Press) 1980; and J. D. Green, *Revolution in Iran: The Politics of Countermobilization*, (Princeton: Princeton University Press) 1982.

10. Israeli culture and politics are too complicated to neatly fit this generalization. Nationalist political parties also draw their support from European-origin, higher-income, and well-educated segments of the Israeli population, and religious fundamentalists include many who are Ashkenazic in background.

Chapter 5. Comparison

1. The *hillula* of Rabbi David u'Moshe is still being held in Morocco in its traditional format. The participants include not only members of

the small Jewish community that remained in Morocco, but also great crowds of persons who now live in France and Israel and return yearly to take part in the celebration.

2. Rabbi Abouhatzeira's son literally inherited his illustrious father's mantle. The fact that he is a "repentant sinner," having among other things spent some years in an Israeli prison, may actually magnify his reputation and powers. He is still a controversial figure and has not yet been entirely accepted as the Baba Sali's successor.

3. Bilu mentions several other new shrines in the making: one of these is located in Kiryat Gat, another in Ofakim. Both are new towns with a high percentage of Moroccan residents.

References

Abeles, M. 1988. "Modern Political Ritual: An Inauguration and a Pilgrimage by President Mitterand," *Current Anthropology* 29: 391-404.

Abitol, M. 1982. *Les Juifs d'Afrique du Nord Sous Vichy*, Paris.

Aronoff, M. 1984. "Gush Emunim," in M. Aronoff, ed., *Political Anthropology* 3: 63-84. New Brunswick, N.J.: Transaction Books.

Aviad, J. 1983. *Return to Judaism: Religious Renewal in Israel*. Chicago: University of Chicago Press.

Bauman, R. 1975. "Verbal Art as Performance," *American Anthropologist* 77, no. 2: 290-311.

Ben-Ami, I. 1977. "The Saint Rabbi Nissim ben Nissim" [Hebrew], *North African Jewry in the Nineteenth and Twentieth Centuries*. Jerusalem: Ben Zvi Institute.

————. 1981. "Folk Veneration of Saints among Moroccan Jews," S. Morag, I. Ben-Ami, and N. Stillman, eds., *Studies in Judaism and Islam*. Jerusalem: Magnes Press.

————. 1984. *Folk Veneration of Saints among the Jews of Morocco* [Hebrew]. Jerusalem: Magnes Press.

Ben-Amos, D., and K. Goldstein. 1975. *Folklore: Communication and Performance*. The Hague: Mouton.

Ben-Ari, E., and Y. Bilu. 1987. "Saints' Sanctuaries in Israeli Development Towns: On a Mechanism of Urban Transformation," *Urban Anthropology* 16, no. 2: 243-72.

Ben-Dor, S. 1987. "The Sigd of Beta Israel: Testimony to a Community in Transition," in M. Ashkenazi and A. Weingrod, eds., *Ethiopian Jews and Israel*, New Brunswick, N.J.: Transaction Books, pp. 140-59.

Bilu, Y. 1984. "Motivation Personelle et Signification Sociale du Phenomene de la Veneration des Saints Parmi les Juifs Morocains en Israel," in J. C. Lasri and C. Rapia eds., *Juifs Nord-Africains D'Ajourdhui*. Montreal: Presses de l'Universite de Montreal.

————. 1987. "Dreams and Wishes of the Saint," in H. Goldberg, ed., *Judaism Viewed from Within and Without*. Albany: State University of New York Press, pp. 285-313.

Chouri, S. 1985. *The Life and Works of Rabbi Chayim Chouri* [Hebrew]. Beersheba: Hemed Press.

Cohen, A. 1980. "Drama and Politics in the Development of a London Carnival," *Man* 15: 66-85.

————. 1982. "A Polyethnic London Carnival as a Contested Cultural Performance," *Ethnic and Racial Studies* 5, no. 1: 23-38.

Cohen, E. 1983. "Ethnicity and Legitimation in Contemporary Israel," *Jerusalem Quarterly*, no. 24: 21-34.

Davis, N. Z. 1984. "Charivari, Honor and Community in Seventeenth Century Lyon and Geneva," in J. MacAloon, ed., *Rite, Drama, Festival, Spectacle*. Philadelphia: ISHI Publications.

Deshen, S. 1974. "Political Ethnicity and Cultural Ethnicity in Israel during the 1960s," in A. Cohen, ed., *Urban Ethnicity*. London: Tavistock Publications.

————. 1977. "Tunisian *Hilluloth*," in M. Shokeid and S. Deshen, eds., *The Generation of Transition* [Hebrew]. Jerusalem: Ben Zvi Institute.

————. 1978. "Israeli Judaism: Introduction to the Major Patterns," *International Journal of Middle East Studies* 9: 141-69.

———— . 1982. "The Social Structure of Southern Tunisian Jewry in the Early 20th Century," in S. Deshen and W. Zenner, eds., *Jewish Society in the Middle East*. Washington, D.C.: University Press of America.

Eickelman, D. 1976. *Moroccan Islam*. Austin: University of Texas Press.

Encyclopedia of Judaism. 1971. Jerusalem: Keter Publishing.

Feldman, E. 1977. *Biblical and Post-Biblical Defilement and Mourning: Law as Theology*. New York: Yeshiva University Press.

Friedman, M. 1985. "The NRP in Transition — Behind the Party's Electoral Decline," in E. Krausz, ed., *Politics and Society in Israel*, pp. 270-97. New Brunswick, N.J.: Transaction Books.

Geertz, C. 1968. *Islam Observed*. New Haven, Conn.: Yale University Press.

———— . 1973. *The Interpretation of Cultures*. New York: Basic Books.

Gellner, E. 1969. *Saints of the Atlas*. Chicago: University of Chicago Press.

Goffman, E. 1959. *The Presentation of Self in Everyday Life*. New York: Anchor Books.

Gluckman, M. 1940. "Analysis of a Social Situation in Modern Zululand," *Bantu Studies*.

———— . 1963. "Rituals of Rebellion in South-East Africa," in *Order and Rebellion in Tribal Africa*, pp. 110-27. London: Cohen and West.

Goldberg, H. 1978. "The Mimouna and the Minority Status of Moroccan Jews," *Ethnology* 17: 75-85.

———— . 1983. "The Mellahs of Southern Morocco," *The Maghreb Review* 9: 61-9.

Goldziher, I. 1971. *Muslim Studies*. Chicago: Aldine Publishers.

Halper, J. and H. Abromovitz. 1984. "The Saharanei Celebration in Kurdistan and Israel," in S. Deshen and M. Shokeid, eds., *Jews of the Middle East* [Hebrew]. Tel Aviv: Shocken Books.

Hazleton, L. 1977. *Israeli Women: The Reality behind the Myths*. New York: Simon and Schuster.

Hedi Hadarom (News of the South) [Hebrew], 1966.

Hymes, D. 1975. "Breakthrough into Performance," in D. Ben-Amos and K. Goldstein, eds., *Communication and Performance*. The Hague: Mouton.

Kapferer, B. 1983. *A Celebration of Demons*. Bloomington: Indiana University Press.

Leibman, C. 1982. "Israel's Civil Religion," *Jerusalem Quarterly* 23: 57-69.

MacAloon, J. 1984. *Rite, Drama, Festival, Spectacle: Rehearsals towards a Theory of Cultural Performance*. Philadelphia: ISHI Publications.

Manning, F. 1983. *The Celebration of Society*. Bowling Green, Ky.: Bowling Green University Popular Press.

Matzliach, A. and R. Chadad. No date. *In the Light of the Living King* [Hebrew].

Peres, Y. 1985. "Horizontal Integration and Vertical Differentiation among Jewish Ethnicities in Israel," in A. Weingrod, ed., *Studies in Israeli Ethnicity*. New York: Gordon and Breach.

Sallnow, M. 1981. "Communitas Reconsidered: The Sociology of Andean Pilgrimage," *Man* 16: 163-82.

Scholem, G. 1954. *Major Trends in Jewish Mysticism*. New York: Shocken Books.

Shokeid, M. 1971. *The Dual Heritage*. Manchester, N.H.: Manchester University Press.

———— (with S. Deshen). 1974. *The Predicament of Homecoming*. Ithaca, N.Y.: Cornell University Press.

————. 1984. "Cultural Ethnicity in Israel: The Case of the Middle Eastern Jews' Ethnicity," *Association for Jewish Studies Review* 9 no. 2: 247-71.

Shuval, J. 1956. "Patterns of Intergroup Tension and Affinity," *International Social Science Bulletin* 8: 75-126.

Singer, M. 1959. *When a Great Tradition Modernizes*. London: Pall Mall.

Spilerman, S. and J. Habib. 1976. "Development Towns in Israel: The Role of Community in Creating Ethnic Disparities in Labor Force Characteristics," *American Journal of Sociology* 81: 781-812.

Stillman, N. A. 1982. "Saddiq and Marabout in Morocco." in I. Ben-Ami, ed., *The Sephardi and Oriental Jewish Heritage*. Jerusalem: Magnes Press.

Turner, Victor W. 1967. *The Forest of Symbols*. Ithaca, N.Y.: Cornell University Press.

————. 1969. *The Ritual Process*. London: Routledge and Kegan Paul.

————. 1982. *Celebration*. Washington, D.C.: Smithsonian Institution Press.

————. 1984. "Liminality and the Performative Genres," in J. MacAloon, ed., *Rite, Drama, Festival, Spectacle*. Philadelphia: ISHI Publications.

————. 1985. "Liminality, Kabbalah and the Media," *Religion* 15.

Udovitch, A., and L. Valensi. 1984. *The Last Arab Jews*. New York: Harwood Academic Publishers.

Van Gennep, A. 1911. *Les Rites de Passage*. Paris.

Vilnai, Z. 1963. *Holy Places in Eretz Yisrael* [Hebrew]. Jerusalem: Rav Kook Press.

Voinot, L. 1949. *Pelerinages Judeo-Musulmans du Maroc*. Paris: Larose.

Warner, W. Lloyd. 1959. *The Living and the Dead*. New Haven, Conn.: Yale University Press.

Weingrod, A. 1979. "Recent Trends in Israeli Ethnicity," *Ethnic and Racial Studies*, no. 2: 55-65.

—————, ed. 1985. *Studies in Israeli Ethnicity: After the Ingathering*. New York: Gordon and Breach.

Weissbrod, L. 1982. "Gush Emunim Ideology—From Religious Doctrine to Political Action," *Middle Eastern Studies* 18: 265-75.

Westermarck, E. 1926. *Ritual and Belief in Morocco*. London: Macmillan and Company.

Wiggins, W. 1982. "They Closed the Town up, Man: Reflections on the Civic and Political Dimensions of Juneteenth," in V. Turner, ed., *Celebrations*. Washington, D.C.: Smithsonian Institution Press.

Yancey, W. et. al. 1976. "Emergent Ethnicity," *American Sociological Review* 41: 391-403.

Zenner, W. 1965. "Saints and Piecemeal Supernaturalism among the Jerusalem Sepharadim," *Anthropological Quarterly* 38.

The shrine, a day before the pilgrimage

The zaddik's grave

Early morning of the pilgrimage

Praying to the zaddik

Exchanging food; one of the rabbi's sons holds a picture of the zaddik

Gathered at the shrine; another of the rabbi's sons pouring arak

Pilgrims with the zaddik's son

Kissing the grave

The shrine in the afternoon

בזמן אמת, נכנס למרד. (בלמנר. ד.)

הדבר הכי חשוב הוא שכזה בשעה מסתדר.

The peak of the performance

Candles burning near the shrine

Relaxing under a tent

A picnic on the gravestones

A peddler selling photographs of saints

A nougat vendor and customer

Revelers on the cemetery path

A women's chorus

A man joins the chorus

Beginning to dance

Dancers and the crowd

The musicians

Index

Abitol, Michel, 6
Abouhatzeira, Rabbi Baruch, 99,
    106, 116n.2. *See also* Baba
    Baruch
Abouhatzeira, Rabbi Israel, 98. *See
    also* Baba Sali
Abouhatzeira, Rabbi Yaacov, 98
Agouim, 15, 96
Alexandria, 98
Aliya l'regel, 9. *See also* Pilgrimage
Antistructural, 51, 52
Aronoff, Myron, 89
Ashkenazim (European Jews), 19,
    72, 84, 99
Aviad, Janet, 89

Baal Haness, Rabbi Meir, 22
Baba Sali, 29, 98-9, 106. *See also*
    Abouhatzeira, Rabbi Israel
Baraka, 13
Bar Yochai, Rabbi Shimon, 22
Beersheba: mayor of, 19, 32, 86;
    military cemetery, 30; munici-
    pal cemetery, 8, 17, 58-9; politi-
    cal party factions, 19; Tunisians
    living in, 17
Ben Ami, Issachar, VII, 15, 16,
    73-5, 85, 94-7, 101
Ben Amos, D., and K. Goldstein, 49
Ben Ari, Eyal, and Yoram Bilu,
    77, 100
Ben Dor, S., 105
Berbers, 2, 3
Beth She'an, 71, 95

Bilu, Yoram, 13, 15, 77-8, 95-6, 98
Bnai Brak, 7

Cemetery: in North African Jewish
    tradition, 59; transformed dur-
    ing pilgrimage, 58-60. *See also*
    Pollution
Chorus, 65
Chouri, Rabbi Chayim: immigration
    to Israel, 7; magical powers,
    21-2, 39-43; how pilgrimage
    developed, 8, 16-22, Tunisian
    background, 2, 4-7. *See also*
    Hillula; *Zaddik*
Chouri family, 19, 25, 26, 27, 35-6,
    86, 90
Cohen, Abner, 107-109
Cohen, Erik, 90
Concensus, 48, 52
Cultural performance, 49, 55, 65.
    See also Performance; Singer,
    Milton

Da Matta, Roberto, 107
Davis, Natalie, 49
David u'Moshe, Rabbi, 15, 95-7
Deshen, Shlomo, 3, 11-12, 39, 76-7
Development towns, 71
Dighet, 3. *See also* Hara Sghira
Dimona, 29, 71
Discord, 48, 52, 63
Durkheimian, 52, 82

Edah, 18, 70, 72. *See also* Ethnic
    Group

Eickelman, Dale, 14, 52
Ethnic group: ceremony of renewal,
    81-2, 85, 93, 101, 105, 107, 111;
    cultural pluralism, 73; organi-
    zation of, 18, 70, 72; politics of,
    87. See also Edah
Ethiopian Jews, 105

Friedman, Menachem, 89
Funeral, in Jewish tradition, 59

Gabes, 4, 5, 16, 38, 41
"Gate of Paradise", 95
Geertz, Clifford, 14, 23, 47
Gellner, Ernest, 14
Georgian Jews, 72
German army, in Tunisia, 6, 41
Gluckman, Max, 76, 81
Goldberg, Harvey, 15, 101, 102
Goldstein, Judith, 104
Goldziher, Ignace, 11

Hacohen, Rabbi David, 4
Hacohen, Rabbi Moshe Khalfon, 4
Halper, Jeff, and Henry Abromo-
    vitz, 104
Hameagel, Rabbi Choni, 22,
    94-5, 98
Hara Kabira, 3
Hara Sghira, 3. See also Dighet
Hasidim, 11, 16
Hatzor, 22, 94
Hazelton, Leslie, 80
Hebron, 1, 10
Hillula: behavior during, 25, 36; as
    ethnic celebration, 81-5; in
    Jewish tradition, 10-12; in
    North African tradition, 14-16;
    new hilluloth in Israel, 95-101;
    political dimensions, 85-91;
    social switchboard, 78-9;
    women participants, 79-81;
    who takes part, 37-9. See also
    Rabbi Chayim Chouri; Zaddik

Hunt, Eva, 107
Hymes, D., 48

Icon, 46
Israel: immigration from Tunisia, 7;
    Independence Day, 22; nation-
    alism and fundamentalism,
    88-91; North African immi-
    grants and ethnicity, 69-73;
    religious orientations, 38-9; Six
    Day War, 72, 88

Jellaba, 29, 32
Jerba, 2-5, 7, 16
Jerusalem, 1, 2, 10, 102
Jewish Agency, 7

Kabbala, 10
Kabbalists, 13
Kaddish prayer, 8, 17, 59
Kadosh, 13, 99. See also Zaddik
Kapferer, Bruce, 49
Kiryat, Gat, 71
Kiryat Shmonah, 71
Kurdish Jews, 104

Labor Party, 87, 89, 90, 104
Lag B'Omer, 22, 24, 75. See also
    Meron
Leibman, Charles, 39
Likud Party, 87, 90
Liminal, 48, 57
Liminality, 50, 57, 66

MacAloon, J., 49
Maimonides, 102
Male-female relations: as contest,
    62; among Jews, 60-1; male
    exclusivity, 62-3; among North
    American Jews, 80; separation
    of women, 62-3
Manning, Frank, 107
Marabout, 13, 14
Mawlid, 11
Mazuz, Rabbi Zaken Moshe, 4

Meron, 22, 24, 30, 75. *See also* Lag B'Omer
Mikva, 26
Mimouna, 101-6
Morocco, saints in, 14-16
Moroccan Jews: ethnic demonstrations, 82-4; experience in Israel, 71-2; at *hillula*, 18, 37; political mobility, 87-8; relations with Tunisians, 64-5. *See also* North African Jews
Moshavim, 71
Multivocal, 1, 23, 66
Musem, 14

Netivoth, 98, 99
North African Jews: in cemetery, 59; at *hillula*, 26, 37. *See also* Moroccan Jews; Tunisian Jews
Notting Hill Carnival: adopted by West Indians, 108; compared with *mimouna*, 110; first stages, 108; Trinidadian elements, 109

Palestine, 10
Performance: "center stage", 56; component elements, 53-5; defined, 48; uses in social science, 48-50
Persian Jews, 104
Pilgrimage, 9, 48, 51, 52. *See also* Aliya l'regel; Hillula
Pluralism, 84
Pollution, 26, 59, 61. *See also* Cemetery
Posters, 20, 24, 86

Ramath Gan, 104
Rastafarianism, 110
Redfield, Robert, 50
Reggae, 110
Rites of passage, 50
Ruz-e-begh, 104

Safed, 1, 10, 22. *See also* Bar Yochai, Rabbi Shimon; Kabbala
Saint: defined, 13; in dreams and visions, 13; hierarchy of, 15; in Islam, 14-15; "saint map", 101. *See also* Chouri, Rabbi Chayim; Zaddik
Sallnow, Michael, 52, 66
Scholem, Gershon, 16
Scenario, 48, 63
Script, 53, 57, 63
Seuda, 35-6, 53, 63
Seherrana, 104
Shokeid, Moshe, 75, 80
Shrine, 12, 20, 24, 56, 90
Sigd, 105
Singer, Milton, 49-50, 55. *See also* Cultural Performance
Spilerman, S., and J. Habib, 100

Talmud, 3, 4, 13, 21
Temple, 9, 10
Tiberias, 22
Touvyahu, David, 19
Traditional, 39
Travelers, 10
Tunis, 7, 41
Tunisian Jews: at *hillula*, 17-19, 24, 35-6, 54, 64-5; relations with Muslims, 7; in southern Tunisia, 5, 6, 8, 18; Zionist movement, 6. *See also* North African Jews

Udovitch, Abram, and Lucette Valensi, 2-4, 16

Van Gennep, A., 50
Vichy French, 6
Voinoit, L., 74
Vows, 43

Wali, 10, 11, 13
Warner, W. Lloyd, 107
Weissbrod, L., 89

Westermark, E., 14
Wiggins, W., 107
World War, Second, 42

Zaddik: in different Jewish tra-
    ditions, 16; defined, 12; in
    Morocco, 15, 74; miracles per-
    formed, 39-40; new in Israel,
    16, 94-9; photograph as icon,
    46. See also Chouri, Rabbi
    Chayim; Kadosh; Saint
Ziyara, 10, 11
Zohar, 11

CPSIA information can be obtained at www.ICGtesting.com
Printed in the USA
BVOW04s0226190115

383911BV00001B/173/P